About Learning

by Bernice McCarthy

Illustrated by Carol Keene

Published by About Learning, Inc.

Acknowledgements
Sounds True Audio, Boulder, Colorado, *Thomas Moore on Creativity* Tape, by permission of Thomas Moore, Wilton, N.H.

Prometheus Books, Amherst, New York for *The Mind's Eye: Visual Thinkers, Gifted People with Learning Difficulties, Computer Images* and *The Ironies of Creativity* by Thomas West. Buffalo, NY, 1991, by permission of Trey M. Bankhead Permissions Editor. Pages 14, 19, 138, 184.

By permission of Rose Merrill for her original poem, "Ambidexterous."

 Printed in the United States of America. Published byAbout Learning, Inc., 1251 N. Old Rand Rd., Wauconda, Illinois 60084. 1-800-822-4628.
First edition.
4MAT® is a registered trademark of About Learning, Inc.

ISBN: 09608992-6-x (cloth)

Edited by Mary Colgan McNamara
Cover and illustrations by Carol Keene

To my children and their children
and my beautiful daughters-in-law,
and all the members of the About Learning team.

CONTENTS

About Learning

This book is about learning.
It describes a natural cycle,
a cycle we go through when we learn.

It is a *cycle*
because it begins with us
and returns to us.

It is *natural*
because it contains
the essential elements of human learning.

It occurs spontaneously,
without conscious intervention,
without our having to think about it.

Some of us are more conscious of it than others
and, when we understand this process,
we improve our learning lives.
We are able to create bigger worlds for ourselves
and for our children.

I offer this book as an explanation
of how learning works
with a guarantee that it will improve
your success as learners
and help to enlarge your lives.

Bernice McCarthy
Barrington, Illinois
Spring, 1996

CHAPTER ONE

About the Natural Cycle

A Learner's Story

Leticia was in first grade and she loved school. She couldn't eat breakfast fast enough in her excitement to get to school. Everything she longed for was present in that world – the teacher's loving interest, the thrill of deciphering the symbols that meant things, things she could touch and feel, the addition facts that the teacher would pose on the board. She could always see the answers; she wondered why some of the children had trouble with theirs.

She even loved the tests. She actually could hardly wait for the tests. Her excitement was like that of the athlete who knows if she can just get her hands on the ball, she can sink it. Each question would burrow in and then open out into an immense space she had never been in before. Each became an exciting foray into even more questions. And as her reading improved, and it did rapidly, she could not get enough of the books, and the table at the back of the room was filled with books! (There were eleven books just about the Land of Oz.)

She welcomed the words and ideas of each new writer to her inner world where she lived in awe and contentment. She thrilled when the teacher told her about ideas people had, ideas that became liquid as she took them to herself. She felt confident, she knew she belonged. Surely her teacher was the smartest person she had ever met and they smiled at each other often throughout the day.

Learning:
To gain knowledge, understanding, skills,
by study, instruction, experience.
— Random House Dictionary

I think what we're seeking
is an experience of being alive.
The life experiences we have resonate within
so we feel the rapture of being alive.
— Joseph Campbell

Watch any child learn,
even the youngest,
perhaps especially the youngest.

What does this child do?
Enters into and is absorbed by what is.
Looks within.
Looks without.
Examines and experiments.

Feels,
puzzles,
tries,
owns –

learns.

Not yet contaminated by fear of failure,
not yet anxious about grades.

When you watch a child learn,
the dynamic is apparent.
Two major things happen –
the child experiences,
and the child reacts to experience.

Reality greets the child
and the child greets reality.

The child is and the child does.

So the pattern of **being someone**,
then reacting to the world **as that someone**,
happens over and over.
This is the learning cycle.

Learning is the making of meaning.
— Robert Kegan

We need to learn how to be someone
as well as how to react to the world.
We need to learn how to learn.

This book is about learning
and it is also my story –
a story of what I have come to understand
about learning.

I have studied learning all my professional life.
I started out studying teaching first;
then I realized I needed to focus on learning
in order to teach.

I attracted the "Hall Rats" to my classrooms,
the kids who hated school
and who acted out their hatred.

Hatred is the wrong word.
I use it because that is how they seemed to us, their teachers.
It was anger, and most of all it was fear,
fear that we were right,
that learning and the good life were only for the favored few,
that there really was something wrong with them.

The real point is to make the case
for the plurality of intellect.
... It is of the utmost importance
that we recognize and nurture
all of the varied human intelligences,
and all of the combinations of intelligences.
— Howard Gardner

I saw smarts in them, lots of smarts.
I mean real smarts, spatial things.
(I did not know what they were then.)
Three-dimensional problem-solving things
that could have translated into skill in higher mathematics,
smarts about how life was,
relationship smarts,
patterning smarts,
smarts that saw the discrepant events,
detective smarts –
knowing when someone was lying,
knowing when someone was fawning,
knowing when someone meant it,
knowing when someone didn't.

I began to learn what learning was
and what it wasn't.
It wasn't just what school taught and thought it was.

Most of all I saw the differences,
the differences in the ways people learn.
And I saw that these differences were good.

The kinds of minds
that children come to own
are profoundly influenced
by the kind of experiences
they are able to secure
in the course of their lives.
... Mind is the product of opportunity.
... We can do a great deal about the conditions
and opportunities the young have
during the course of their development.
— Elliot Eisner

Each of us is truly unique
because we form ourselves.

We are not born with our minds.
We have to construct them,
to make them something that blends
all that we bring
with all we encounter,
do,
are done to,
invite,
reject,
and especially hope.

It is so important to understand this.
We construct our minds.

We need people to help us –
to move us from where we are
to where we can be.
Learning is a social act, we are in relationship.
We go out to the world.
The world does not only come in on us.
No.
We react, we confront, we resolve.
We create and transform.

But first we have to realize
we are somebody.

After "A Nation at Risk"
millions of meaningless new tests
consumed the time of students.
Those youngsters who did badly
on these tests, and who, along with their teachers,
already knew they were doing badly,
received a new and destructive infusion of discouragement
in the form of low test scores followed by mindless tracking.
In the name of "standards" they were taken off the assembly line
and put on lower tracks for repairs – a strategy that most often
failed to restore either their learning or their motivation to learn.
— Harold Howe II

So I began with learning styles
because they are the most obvious differences one finds in teaching.

I also saw clearly that only certain kinds of learners
were honored in our schools.

The others, and there were many of those,
including myself,
were dishonored.

The dishonored ones find it hard to believe that they are somebody.

Intrigued by the work of David Kolb and Kurt Lewin,
I began with the two major elements in how people learn –
how we **perceive**,
how we are in and take in experience,

and how we **process**,
how we react, confront and resolve
and become the creators
we are meant to be.

Lewin named these two moments,
these two movements,
perceiving (The child is who s/he is in experience.)
and processing. (The child does.)
It is crucial to understand how these two movements
function in our lives.

Picture the learning cycle as a clock.
Learning starts at 12 o'clock and continues around the clock
forward to the next 12 o'clock.
The two dimensions of perceiving and processing form this cycle.

Visualize the first dimension, perceiving, as a line running from
12 o'clock to 6 o'clock.

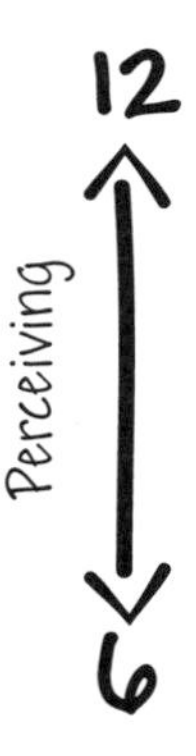

This line represents perception, *how we take in* the things we learn.

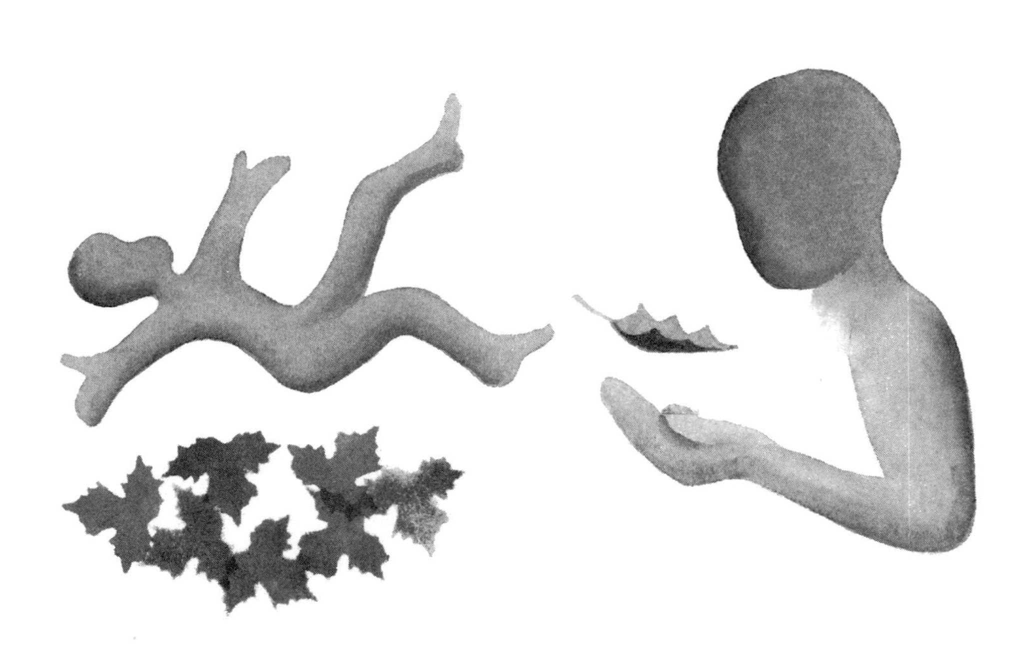

Visualize the second dimension as a line running from 3 o'clock to 9 o'clock.

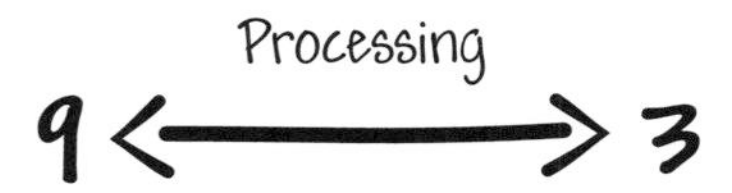

This line represents processing, *what we do* with what we take in.

So learning grows out of this natural rhythm of perceiving and processing, the taking in and giving out, like the way our hearts pump, the diastole and systole of learning.

Being in it.

Being apart from it.

Perceiving

Examine perception,
the 12 o'clock to 6 o'clock line.

We perceive in two ways.
We sense and feel our experiences, the 12 o'clock place,
and then we think our experiences, the 6 o'clock place.

First we sense and feel.
When we run into something new,
something that intrigues us, invades us,
we literally go into it,
we grasp the experience,
we become embedded in it,
we are present in the now.

Then, as we reflect,
we move to **thinking about it**.
We have to move away,
separating ourselves
in order to understand, to intellectualize it,
to structure it.
That is how we deal with newness.
We place it somewhere that connects it
to past knowing.
We need to order it for ourselves,
so we can place it in our world.

12 sensing/feeling

↕

6 thinking

Those who are accustomed
to judge by feeling
do not understand the process of reasoning
because they want to comprehend at a glance,
and are not used to seeking for first principles.

Those who are accustomed
to reason from first principles
do not understand matters of feeling at all,
because they look for first principles
and are unable to comprehend at a glance.
— Blaise Pascal

Some of us favor and trust
the sensing/feeling way of perceiving
more than the thinking way.

Others trust the thinking way
more than the sensing/feeling way.

This favoring makes a great difference
in how we go about learning.

Perception is **direct** at 12 o'clock.
We sense and feel newness.
It is immediate.

Perception is **indirect** at 6 o'clock.
Our thinking self takes over, plays the major role.
Our intellect mediates.

Rather than sensing and feeling the newness,
we think it,
we name it,
we classify it,
we abstract it,
we make it a general example of a specific case.

And so we come to understand it that way.
We think it in time.

Wisdom is oftentimes nearer
when we stoop
than when we soar.
— William Wordsworth

Both ways of perceiving are valuable
(not only valuable, but necessary).
After we experience, we need to order our experiences,
to make sense of them,
to name and classify them,
to anchor them in our consciousness,
in the place where we live.

We do this by forming pictures
and ideas about them.
We conceptualize them, we construct images of things.
These conceptualizations are grounded in our experiences,
very unique to us,
very personal,
because we see from behind our own eyes.
Our concepts are our ways of interpreting our world.

Experiencing

Conceptualizing

And so we begin at 12 o'clock
with experience
and we move to 6 o'clock
to order that experience
by conceptualizing it.

This is our dilemma –
in order to taste and not to know
or to know and not to taste –
or more strictly, to lack
one kind of knowledge
because we are in an experience
or to lack another kind
because we are outside it.
As thinkers we are cut off
from what we think about;
as tasting, touching, willing, loving, hating,
we do not clearly understand.
The more lucidly we think,
the more we are cut off:
the more deeply we enter into reality,
the less we can think.
You cannot study Pleasure in the moment
of the nuptial embrace.
— C. S. Lewis

Scholars have used many different words and phrases to describe these two aspects of perception.

12 o'clock

Apprehension (Dewey)	Emotion (Damasio)
Sensory (Piaget)	Eros (Moore)
Intuiting (Bruner)	Subject (Kegan)
Perception (Jung)	One's Reality (Kincheloe and Steinberg)
Intuitive Apprehension (Schopenhauer)	Heart (Caap)
Inspiration (Nietzsche)	Connected personal knowing, "kennen" (Belenky *et. al.*)
Synchronicity – overall meaning (Peat)	Empathy – absorbed into works of art (Worringer)
Nonverbal (Polanyi)	Sensing/Feeling (McCarthy)
Concrete and Direct Experience (Kolb and Hunt)	
Comprehension (Dewey)	Reason (Damasio)
Representative (Piaget)	Logos (Moore)
Analyzing (Bruner)	Object (Kegan)
Judgment (Jung)	A derivative sign language (Kincheloe and Steinberg)
Conceptual, abstract – somewhat lifeless (Schopenhauer)	Head (Caap)
Order, conceptual thought, requiring separation (Nietzsche)	Separate knowing, "wissen" (Belenky *et. al.*)
Analysis, concentration on details (Peat)	Abstraction – discover form and order, detached (Worringer)
Verbal (Polanyi)	Thinking (McCarthy)
Abstract Conceptualizaton (Kolb and Hunt)	

6 o'clock

Opposites cannot be understood without opposites.
— Plato

For us, in the beginning it was being,
and only later was it thinking.

We are and then we think,
and we think only inasmuch as we are,
since thinking is indeed caused
by the structures and operations of being.
— Antonio Damasio

The tension between these two ways of perceiving
is the central dynamic in learning.
Real learning is achieved only through a balance
between the two.

Those of us who favor the sensing/feeling dimension
need to understand the beauty and order of thinking.
And those who move to thinking too quickly
need to linger in the sensing and feeling of things –
percepts and concepts, experiencing and conceptualizing.

The most important issue in all of this
is the issue of growth, of learning itself.

Unless we move out of experience,
out of the 12 o'clock place, into ordering our experiences,
understanding what happens to us
by classifying and naming,
we never learn, we never grow.

It is the act of moving from our feelings to our thoughts
that gets us from **being in** our perceptions
to being able to **see the perceptions** themselves.
We cannot make our perceptions the object of our attention
if we are embedded in them, if we do not balance
our lives with both the 12 o'clock and the 6 o'clock things.

By moving from the 12 o'clock feeling place
to the 6 o'clock thinking place,
we can focus on how we are separate from our perceptions,
how we can differentiate ourselves from them.

How can I tell what I think
till I see what I say?
— E. M. Forster

When I feel sudden anger, I am in it, I actually am anger.
This is the 12 o'clock place.

What if I stop then and ask, what am I angry about?
Why in the world has this person suddenly roused me to such intense feeling?
Why have I lurched into this red, feverish place?
What old happening is happening here again?

When I do that, I make my anger the object of my thought.
This is the 6 o'clock place.
Then I can learn from that anger.
I can stand outside of it to know the inside of it better.

Conceptual thought demands separation
of thinking from feeling,
of object from subject.
— Anthony Storr

So the real issue in learning
is how to balance being subject to our feelings
with relating to our feelings as object,
how to lose an old center of self
in order to discover a new wiser one,
how to continually move around the cycle.

We perceive all newness
by connecting it to oldness.

Think of a flower standing in the sun,
standing in the rain,
being in life,
taking in nutrients,
absorbing from the soil, the air.

That is how perception begins and moves within.

As humans we need then to go on,
to **put** the new learning somewhere.

As we begin to learn it,
we must enfold it into the things we already know.

And so we name it,
and the naming,
whether what the experts call it, or we call it,
or some combination of both,
makes it more specifically accessible to us.

If all meanings
could be adequately expressed by words,
the arts of painting and music
would not exist.
— John Dewey

Once named,
the world in its turn reappears
to the namers as a problem
and requires of them
a new naming.
— Paulo Freire

But the name is never the thing.
No reality can ever be adequately described in words.

Words are derivative sign language about real things.
They are not the same as the real things.

The mistake of thinking
that words are the real things
causes all kinds of trouble
because words are never enough.

Galaxies are not just lists.
Flowers are not just genus classifications.
Geography is not just maps.

To make a name a nest,
to stay in thinking,
to use naming as an ending
rather than as understanding,
is hazardous to learning.
It elevates one station of the cycle
over the cycle itself.
We must move back up to feeling –

from our feelings,
to our thoughts,
and back to new and richer perceptions,
greater and deeper feelings,
greater because they are more informed,
deeper because we have faced ourselves
and learned about ourselves.

Eros: *relatedness, love, intimacy, longing, attraction,*
desire, interest, wish attachment, a communal sense,
and the pleasure not of distance, but of closeness

Logos: *word, logic, understanding, language, form,*
definitions, classifying, reflecting from a distance,
to stand back and look

These two things work together in the best of worlds,
two principles of life that intertwine,
in our times, often split apart, alienating our lives.

The notion that Eros is worthy of our attention,
of the same consideration we give to Logos,
to understanding,
means we can live creatively
and from a very profound source.

Imagine if the goal of teaching students
about the animal world
was that they would love animals more
as well as understand them better.
— Thomas Moore

In his marvelous reflections on creativity,
Thomas Moore passionately describes the distortion caused
when understanding (Logos) is split off from love (Eros),
when our theories become the only truth,
when we even punish people who do not agree
with our way of understanding the world.

When we do not return to 12 o'clock.

Each new 6 o'clock understanding
needs to return to 12 o'clock love
in order to be complete and to continue to grow.

To learn from our experience,
we need both kinds of perception –
the sensing/feeling acts of the heart
and the conceptualized words and pictures of the head.

Real learning transforms.

If our lives are to become transformed,
we must experience and understand
how the wheel turns,
the interplay of the perceiving
and processing dimensions
of the natural learning cycle.

To know the world
we must construct it.
— Pavese

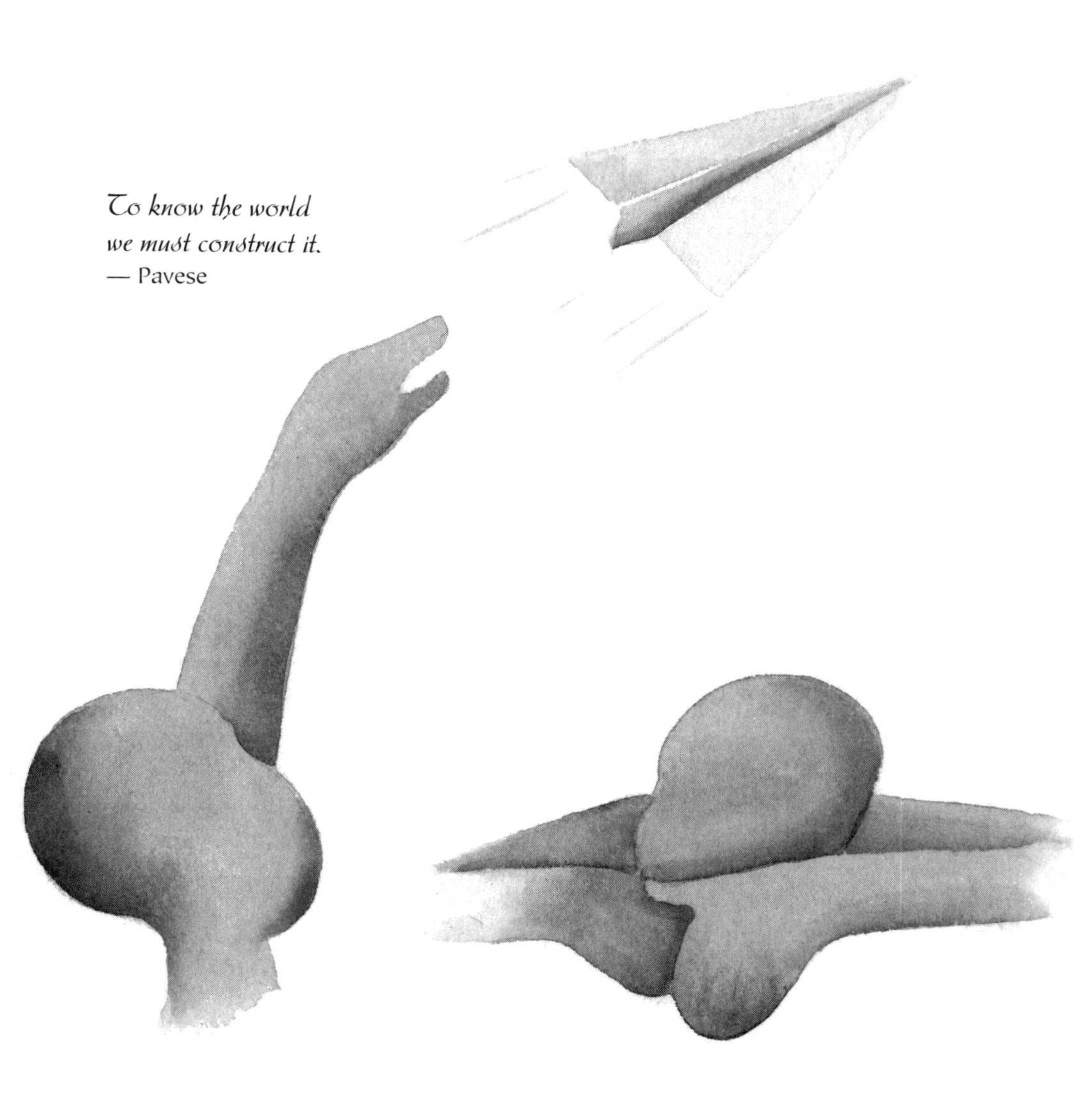

Processing

In addition to perceiving, taking things in,
we must do something with them
if we are to truly learn them.

And, so we process what we learn,
we deal with it in some way that helps us to use it
and to integrate it
so it becomes a permanent part of our lives.

And as with perception,
we process in two ways.

We reflect on our experience
and we act on that reflection.

We watch and we do.

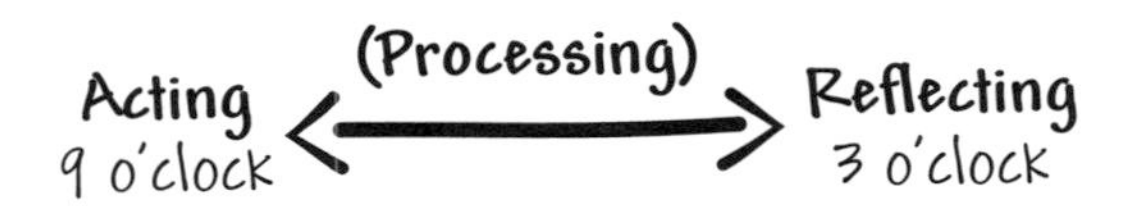

If it isn't used,
it isn't learned.
— Aleksandr Luria

We reflect on it, watch it,
see how we feel about it,
dialogue with others
and with ourselves
about its meaning.

We go inside ourselves
to check it out with the person we are,
we filter it through ourselves.

If I am to create meaning from my reflections,
I need to act on them.
I need to do something with the results of my watching –
to take it to use,
to extend those reflections into some testing place,
into trying,
into tinkering.
And then to reflect anew on those tinkerings.

Insight: *apprehending through intuitive understanding,*
seeing underlying characteristics, inner truth
of mullings and ponderings over time

Outsight: *enlivening, enhancing, discovering,*
making one's own… in the real world –
by virtue of gracing it
with this-or-that private image

— Richard Jones

Scholars have used many different words
to describe these two aspects of what I am referring to as processing.

9 o'clock	**3 o'clock**
Environmental, interacting with... (Dewey)	Personal, interacting with... (Dewey)
Extraversion (Jung)	Introversion (Jung)
Extension (Kolb)	Intention (Kolb)
Active Experimentation (Lewin)	Reflective Observation (Lewin)
Outsight (Jones)	Insight (Jones)
Achieving (Macmurray)	Imagining (Macmurray)
Practical and Scientific (Moustakas)	Contemplative and Aesthetic (Moustakas)
Extratensive (Rorschach)	Intratensive (Rorschach)
Action Mode (Diekman)	Receptive Mode (Diekman)
Doing (McCarthy)	Reflecting (McCarthy)

Nothing takes root in mind
when there is no balance
between doing and receiving.
— John Dewey

Life is real only in the full rhythm between these two.
— John Macmurray

As with sensing/feeling and thinking,
reflecting and doing need to be in balance.
Dewey, Macmurray, and many others stress this need for balance.

When we reflect on our actions,
we confer intentionality on them.

By taking a look at what we actually do,
not just what we think we do,
we come to see the discrepancies.

We raise our consciousness
from an unexamined place
to a meaning place where deliberate actions can follow,
where we can change our behavior
for real reasons.

Macmurray emphasizes that we make what we do
deliberate and intentional.

When we confer intentionality on our actions,
we raise our watching to significance –
significance because our reflections
help to give us purpose.
How we feel, what we value, and how we act
move together in synchronicity.

Reflecting on our actions confers intentionality

Acting, achieving ______________ Reflecting, imagining

Within the word
we find two dimensions …
reflection and action…
if one is sacrificed
even in part
the other immediately suffers.
To speak a true word
is to transform the world.
— Paulo Freire

Balancing reflecting and acting
transforms.

We take our experiences from the world,
the world outside, the world that does things to and with us,

and we deal with them in our real world,
our own world,
the world inside.

Facts become possibilities,
and existence becomes purposeful,
and meaning and action move together.
We interact with the world in our way.

When we reflect deeply and honestly,
when we subject our actions to thoughtful examination,
when we act with purpose,
not whim or thoughtlessness,
we imbue our actions with meaning.

I believe this balanced rhythm is the essence
of a life lived with grace.

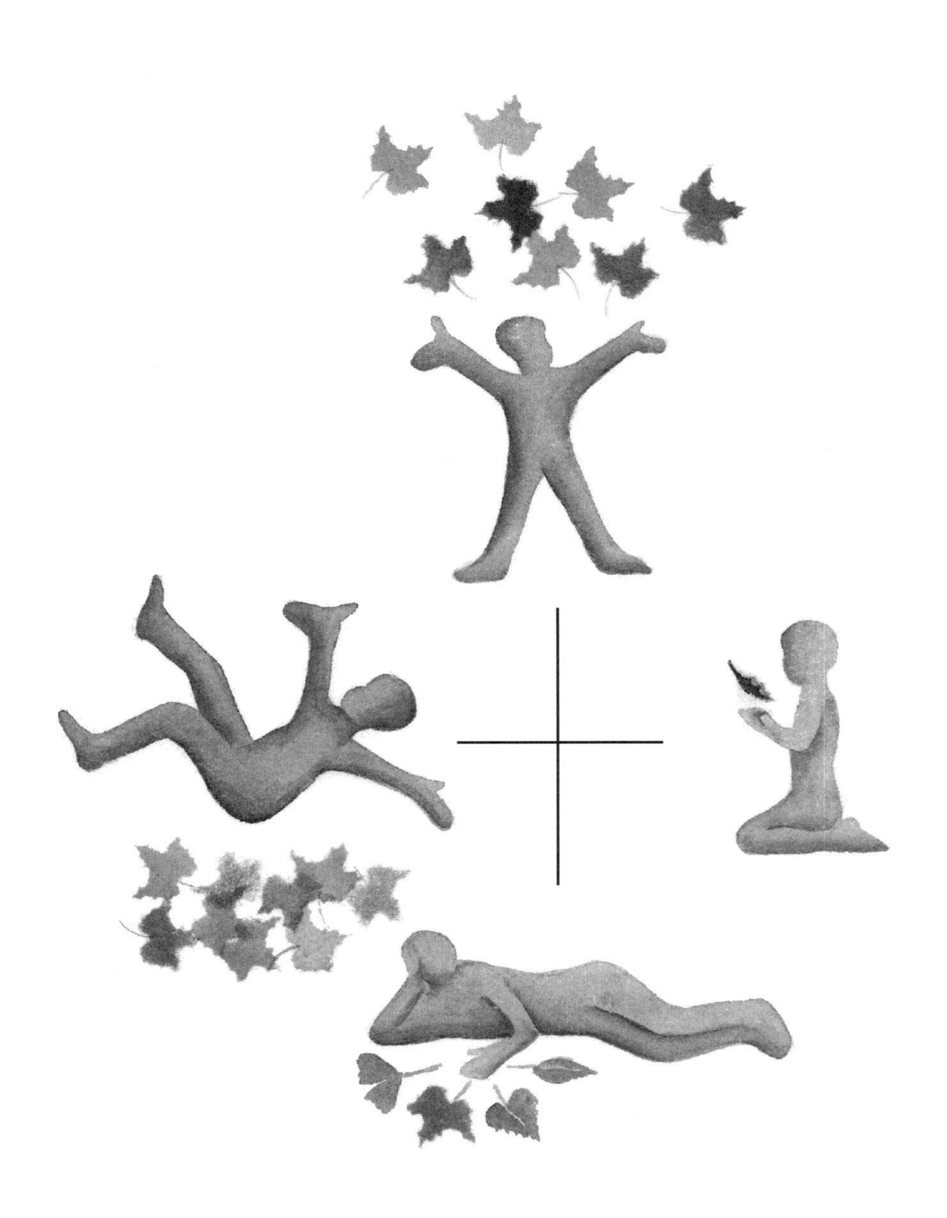

Putting the Two Dimensions Together

To combine perceiving
(taking things in)
with processing
(doing something with them)
creates a natural learning cycle.

Relating perceiving and processing, as Kurt Lewin did,
overlaying the 3 to 9 o'clock dimension
upon the 12 to 6 o'clock dimension,
uncovers a cycle
that contains the essential elements
of learning:
sensing/feeling, reflecting,
thinking, and doing,
the vantage points of human consciousness.

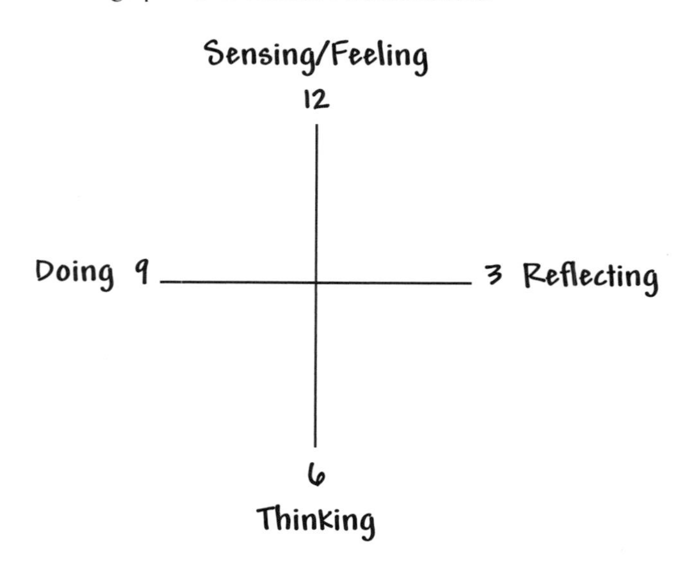

This overlay creates a process
that begins with the self
and returns back to the self.

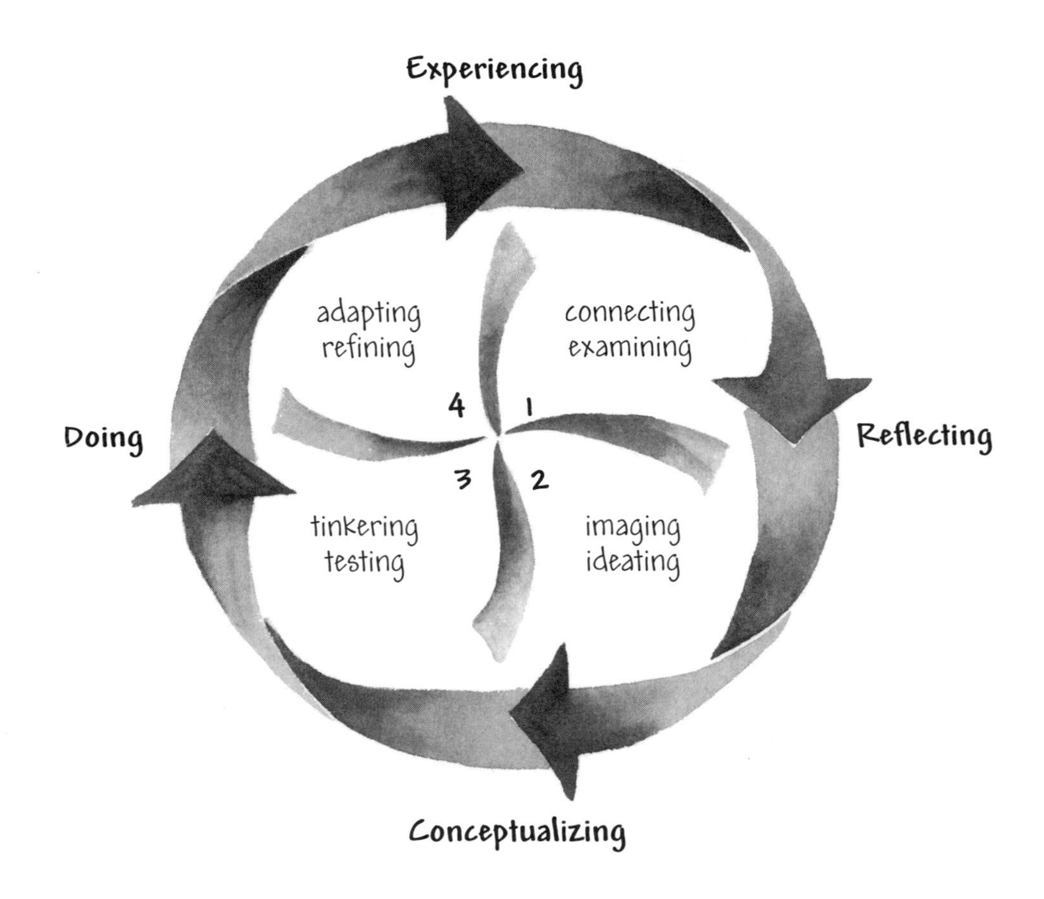
Experiencing
Reflecting
Conceptualizing
Doing
adapting
refining
connecting
examining
4
1
3
2
tinkering
testing
imaging
ideating

I start with my experience at 12 o'clock,
with how I sense and feel the world.

Next I reflect.
Not only do I watch what's happening,
but I examine how I feel about what's happening,
I watch myself. This is the 3 o'clock place,
the filtering place.

Then I conceptualize what's happening,
I image it, I ideate it, I name it.
I listen, I examine what the experts say,
I put this together with what I know.
This is the 6 o'clock place.

Acting on it, I refine, I edit.
This is the 9 o'clock place.
I adapt it, I make it mine.
Then it is learned.
Only then is it integrated into my life.

Learning is not whole or complete
until we get back around to 12:00.

The more we learn,
the more unique we become.
— Renata Caine

So learning begins with me,
my connections to my experience,
and it ends when I adapt my ponderings of it,
my examinings,
my use of it
in my life –
it comes back to me.

It isn't only "me" I'm dealing with.
There are other voices operating in this process.
Along the way I have reflected and listened –

first to my own voice
striving to blend today with yesterday,

and then to the voices of others,
some with knowledge,
some with nonsense,
speaking of what is known and what they know.

If I have listened, if I have come to understand their way
and learned to distinguish the true from the false,
I can blend these voices with mine
and come finally to the place I need to be,
to the place where I speak in my own voice.

And my voice will have balance,
the balance that comes
from blending outside knowing
with inside knowing.

Through listening and pondering their truths
and melding them with my own,
I will have more of myself.

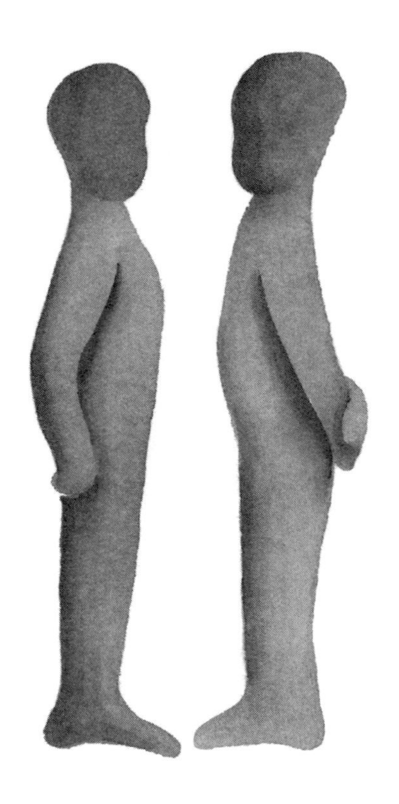

The major purpose of this book
is to help readers use this cycle more consciously,
to pay attention to its parts,
to bring balance and wholeness to learning.

If we follow the clock metaphor,
we realize we can only get
from 12 o'clock to 6 o'clock
by going through 3 o'clock.
And
we can only get back up to 12 o'clock
from 6 o'clock
by going through 9 o'clock.

When I meet you and am intrigued by you,
I go to my **self**, my person, to feel how I feel about you,
the 3 o'clock place.

I reflect on you,
I dialogue with others and with myself
about what meaning you might have for me.

I move to 6 o'clock to name you,
I may call you friend, or confidante, or fellow traveler,
(and the naming is always inadequate).

Then I "use" you, as my friend, as my confidante,
and in the using, the 9 o'clock place,
I come to know you in another way,
as someone to do things with, to act with.

And so I return to 12 o'clock, now knowing you in many ways,
through experience, through reflection,
by naming, through doing with and then back to being.

Everything we do consciously remains for us.
— Gurdjieff and Ouspinsky

Now you are integrated into my life
and, if our relationship is to be forever new,
we must continue around that cycle,
never taking anything for granted,
never stuck with the same names,
never doing only the same things,
unless they continue to bring newness to us.

We must rather always open
to what each of us is becoming.

If I ever believe I really know you,
I demean you with my limitations.

And so the learning, my knowing of you,
must continue around the cycle,
moving to higher levels of experiencing and knowing
by reflecting and acting anew.

Find a way
to engage the heart
in the problem
and you are likely to see
the child rise naturally
to his own optimal levels
of uncertainty,
risk and relevance.
— Richard Jones

We start from where we live,
from behind our eyes,
in the way we see things,
in the way we feel things
with our hearts.
This is the place of our personal knowing.

We rely on our senses.
We begin to develop intuitions we can trust,
grounded in our experiences.

We build on the known as we move to the unknown,
to deeper beliefs, to changes
because the cycle spirals.

It is critical to remember that it begins with Feeling,
with Eros, with Apprehension, with Heart,
with Intuition, with Emotion, with Connectedness,
with Empathy, with Subjectivity, with One's Reality.

If our **experiencing**, our 12 o'clock, has meaning,
we reflect on it,
we ponder it,
we feel how we feel,
we interiorize it.

Think of this **reflecting, this interiorizing** as 3 o'clock.

Our reflections take us to concepts –
first we image them, see pictures of them in our minds,
then we name them and develop theories about them.

Think of this **conceptualizing** as 6 o'clock.

Next we try our theories
in order to test them,
to corroborate, verify, authenticate.
We see things in light of our theory,
we become aware of them while using them,
we begin to understand how they work.

Think of this **doing** as 9 o'clock.

And if something works,
if it makes useful sense,
we integrate it into our lives.

Then, and only then, have we learned it.
In this cycle we blend intent and content into significance.

*Personal participation
is the universal principle
of knowing.*
— Michael Polanyi

Think about reading.

Your goal when you read is to understand,
to construct meaning as you go along.
You pause for a moment
needing to look away from the page.
You connect relevant background information,
you attend to the content,
you evaluate the gist,
comparing it with what you already know.
You construct how it could have use in your life,
you draw inferences, interpreting what you read.

And if the reading has had meaning,
you add it to your knowledge repertoire.
You go through the cycle.

Think about falling in love.

You are totally into feeling at first.
Then you reflect,
especially when your friends ask,

"What's s/he like?"

You begin classifying, naming
friend, confidante, advisor, partner…

Then you use your lover as friend,
confidante, advisor, partner,
and if that person remains in all unique humanness
those things for you,
then you integrate that relationship into your life.
You move from subjectivity to objectivity to integration.

You only really know love
when you have completed this cycle
and completed it many times over.

Cycle: *A single complete execution*
of a periodically repeated phenomenon

Spiral: *A curve on a plane*
that winds around a fixed center point
at a continuously increasing
distance from the point

These cycles are really spirals.

As we move around the cycle,
we increase our distance and depth
from the starting point.
We get better and better at all of it.

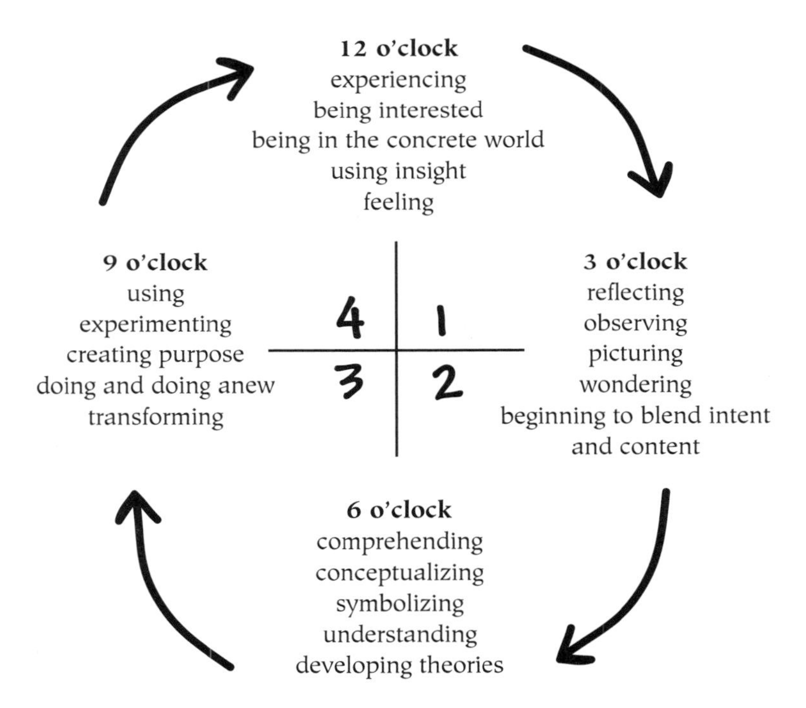

The patterns and combinations we choose
and favor over time
create our learning preferences.

We have a right to our own learning preferences,
our favorite places on the cycle.

But clearly to be whole
we all need to do all of it.

Learning is a from-to experience.
We go from ourselves to the newness.
It is not automatic.
It is the act of a person, the knower,
forming the integration.
The learner attends and intends.

You begin with your feelings, your subjectivity,
bringing all of who you are at that moment to the act,
beginning the process of internalizing what has happened,
pondering, musing,
separating yourself from your feelings
in order to look at your feelings.

You move to naming, conceptualizing,
in order to understand, to be objective,
to organize what you encounter for future use.

You try out the new learning, refine it, edit it,
and, in using it your way, you integrate it.

At that moment, the moment of integration,
learning happens.

It is a meaning-making process,
one by which we create our minds
and construct our lives.
It is continuous, ongoing.
It is a self-renewing cycle.

Like a Greek dance,
the circle never closes.

CHAPTER TWO

About Different Kinds of Learners

A Learner's Story

Linda was in sixth grade when she hit the wall on math. She had loved school up until then—loved every teacher. She even hung around the school during summer vacation to help out the teachers who stayed on when school was closed. Her teachers and classmates agreed that her poetry was really quite good, and it often appeared in local publications. But math was a real problem. She couldn't make it connect to anything. She simply could not see the patterns. When she was a junior in college, a new professor arrived on campus. The word was out that he was sharp and a great teacher. On the day before her statistics class, she met him in the hall and he said, "Oh, you're Linda, I've been reading your poetry. You are going to do very well in statistics." She questioned him in amazement, "How can you say that? I have such difficulty in all my math classes." He smiled and answered, "I can tell from your poetry that you understand symmetry. Statistics is about symmetry. As a matter of fact statistics is the poetry of math."

Linda went on to make an A+ in that class. Her professor connected statistics to her life, he showed her the patterns. She still has a sense of great loss about her school math and says algebra was worse than the dentist. But geometry and that one statistics class shine in her memory as connected to her and her life because her teachers taught her to see the patterns.

If a man does not keep pace with his companions,
perhaps it is because he hears a different drummer.
Let him step to the music he hears,
however measured and far away.
— Henry David Thoreau

Like a Greek dance,
the circle is born of the ordinary things of life –
living within the moment (12 o'clock),
finding meaning (3 o'clock),
understanding (6 o'clock),
and making a difference with our doing (9 o'clock).

In the dance of learning,
each person knows the music
and follows an inner urging to the step.

Each travels the cycle,
but some parts of it feel more natural,
suit us better.
These are the places where we tend to linger.

Some of us linger in
the 12 o'clock feeling place,
where we process through our very skin,
filled with the moment, open to the sensations –

some of us linger in the 3 o'clock reflecting place,
where we feel how we feel,
processing with ponderings and musings,
open to our inner quiet –

some of us linger in the 6 o'clock thinking place,
where we stand back from and examine and name,
converging on the meaning –

some of us linger in the 9 o'clock doing place,
where we tinker and explore, and act and accomplish,
creating the outcome.

A trifling matter,
and fussy of me,
but we all have our little ways.
— A.A. Milne

This lingering makes a great difference
in the way we learn,
a difference that profoundly affects
how things go for us
in school, at work,
in relationships,
and in life.

The comfort we experience
at certain places in the cycle
creates patterns –
patterns that influence the way we approach newness,
the way we deal with ambiguity,
the types of shadow things we tend to avoid,
the speed with which we move to judgment,
the depth of our reflections,
the boldness of our actions.

Our favorite place or places to hang around on this cycle
form our unique learning style.

People who like to linger in sensing/feeling and watching
have a particular learning style.

These people are in what I call the first quadrant,
the 12 o'clock to 3 o'clock place,
bounded by sensing/feeling at 12 o'clock
and reflecting at 3 o'clock.
I call them **Type One Learners.**

Because they sense and feel
and reflect on their experiences,
they are outstanding observers of people,
highly imaginative,
at home with their feelings,
believers in their experience,
listeners par excellence,
caring nurturers,
and people committed to making the world a better place.

People who like to linger in watching and thinking
have a particular learning style.

These people are in the second quadrant,
the 3 o'clock to 6 o'clock place,
bounded by reflecting and thinking.
I call them **Type Two Learners.**

Because they reflect on their experiences,
analyze them, classify, think them,
they are outstanding conceptualizers of content,
highly organized,
at home with details and data,
believers in their ability to understand,
planners par excellence,
concerned about structure,
and committed to making the world more lucid.

People who like to linger in thinking and doing
have a particular learning style.

These people are in the third quadrant,
the 6 o'clock to 9 o'clock place,
bounded by thinking and doing.
I call them **Type Three Learners.**

Because they think about theory
and act to apply it,
they are outstanding problem-solvers,
highly productive,
at home with tasks and deadlines,
believers in their ability to get the job done,
operationalizers par excellence,
concerned about productivity,
and committed to making the world work better.

People who like to linger in doing and sensing/feeling
have a particular learning style.

These people are in the fourth quadrant,
the 9 o'clock to 12 o'clock place,
bounded by doing and sensing/feeling.
I call them **Type Four Learners.**

Because they embrace their experiences
and act to extend and enrich them,
they are outstanding entrepreneurs,
highly energetic,
at home with ambiguity and change,
believers in their ability to influence what happens,
risk-takers par excellence,
concerned about growth and renewal,
and committed to challenging the boundaries their worlds create.

The perceiving dimension,
from 12 o'clock to 6 o'clock,
is a continuum that ranges
from the rawness of feeling
to the ripeness of thought.

Those who perceive in a sensing/feeling way,
the Type Ones and the Type Fours, project themselves
into the reality of the now, the immediate.
They tend to the actual experience itself.
They immerse themselves directly,
they perceive primarily through their senses.
They intuit.

Those who approach experience in a thinking way,
the Type Twos and the Type Threes, tend to mediate perception,
to distance the self from the senses,
to create the abstract.
Their intellect makes the first real appraisal
and they trust it more than they do their feelings.

While our individual ways of grasping things
are usually the best ways for us,
all learners need to do both
for the fullest possible understanding of experience.

The processing dimension,
from 3 o'clock to 9 o'clock,
is a continuum that ranges
from the need to internalize
to the need to act.

The Reflectors,
the **Type One** and **Type Two** Learners,
refine their interiorizing gifts continually,
but they also need to develop more dash in experimenting and trying.

And the Doers,
the **Type Three** and **Type Four** Learners,
keep polishing their experimenting
and risk-taking acts,
but they also need to develop
more patience, more reflection on their actions.

These combinations of perceiving and processing
result in favoritisms
that form four very different approaches to learning.
And it is to the detailed descriptions of these differences
that we now turn.
These descriptions are presented as they apply
to learning, to teaching, to leading, and to parenting.

Learning Style Characteristics

TYPE ONE: THE IMAGINATIVE LEARNERS

As **learners** they perceive information concretely and process it reflectively.

They integrate experience with the self.

They learn by listening and sharing ideas.

They value insight thinking.

They view their experiences from many perspectives.

They love harmony and work diligently to bring it to the lives of the people around them, both personally and professionally.

They are committed to whatever task they undertake and seek commitment in others.

They are fascinated with people and cultures.

They absorb reality.

They need clarity in their lives.

And meaning is first and foremost what they seek as learners.

Sometimes their feelings interfere with their common sense.

As **teachers** they are primarily interested in helping their students achieve personal growth.

Self-awareness is a major goal they have for their students.

They organize curricula whenever possible to help learners become more authentic human beings.

They see knowledge as assisting growth toward self-actualization.

They organize group work and discussions and encourage honest feedback about feelings.

They organize cooperative studying.

They focus on meaningful goals.

As **leaders** they take the time to help employees develop good ideas.

They tackle problems by reflecting alone and then brainstorming with staff.

They lead with their heart and involve others in decision-making.

They exercise authority through trust and participation.

They work for organizational solidarity, in dialogue with staff concerning the mission.

They need staff who are supportive and share their sense of vision.

As **parents** they try to facilitate self-actualization with their children.

They help their children become more self-aware.

They believe learning should enhance the ability to know one's self and one's place in the world.

They see knowledge as enhancing personal meaning and relationships.

They actively encourage speaking about feelings.

They conduct family discussions with honest and realistic feedback.

They try to engage family members in cooperative efforts.

They help their children identify meaningful goals.

They see discipline as necessary to help their children understand life.

They tend to worry excessively and sometimes are too easygoing.

STRENGTH: Nurturing spirit and imaginative ideas

FUNCTION BY: Clarifying values

GOALS: To be involved in important issues and to bring harmony

FAVORITE QUESTION: Why?

TYPE TWO: THE ANALYTIC LEARNER

As **learners** they perceive information
abstractly and process it reflectively.

They form theories and concepts
by integrating their observations with
what they know.

They seek coherence and continuity.

They strive to know what the experts think.

They learn by carefully reflecting on and
thinking through what they are learning.

They are great detail people.

They work sequentially.

They critique data and information.

They are thorough and industrious
and will reexamine facts assiduously
until they understand.

Schools are designed for the particular
way they learn.

They try to maximize certainty and
are uncomfortable with subjectivity.

Sometimes they cannot see the forest for the trees.

As **teachers** they are primarily interested
in transmitting knowledge.

They strive to know their content well,
to be scholarly.

They believe curricula should further
understanding of significant information
and should be presented systematically
and should deepen comprehension.

They encourage outstanding learners.

They like their students to present detailed
facts precisely and sequentially.

They believe in the rational use of authority.

As **leaders** they assemble facts and data into coherent theories.

They tackle problems with logic.

They lead by principles and procedures.

They exercise authority with assertive
persuasion, knowing the facts.

They work to enhance their organization
as an embodiment of tradition and prestige.

They need staff who are well organized,
have things down on paper, and
follow through on decisions quickly and precisely.

As **parents** they want their children
to know the important knowledge.

They try to help their children to be as
accurate as possible.

They believe learning should deepen understanding
of significant information and be presented systematically.

They want their children to understand
how the world works.

They encourage their children to be
outstanding lifelong learners.

They provide a structured and organized
home environment.

They seek to help their children love knowledge.

They believe diligence and organization are
necessary for success.

They see discipline as necessary to enable their children
to understand the kind of behavior society expects.

They tend to be rigid and sometimes
discourage original, creative thinking.

STRENGTH: Creating concepts and models

FUNCTION BY: Thinking things through

GOALS: Intellectual recognition

FAVORITE QUESTION: What?

TYPE THREE: THE COMMON SENSE LEARNER

As **learners** they perceive information
abstractly and process it actively.

They integrate theory and application.

They learn by testing theories
and applying common sense to them.

They are pragmatic–if something works, use it.

They are down-to-earth problem-solvers
who resent being given answers.

They do not stand on ceremony, but
get right to the point.

They have a limited tolerance for fuzzy ideas.

They value strategic thinking.

They are skills oriented.

They like to experiment and tinker
with ideas and things.

They instinctively understand how
things work.

They edit reality, cut right to the heart of things.
Sometimes they seem bossy and impersonal.

As **teachers** they are primarily interested
in productivity and competence.

They strive to give their students the skills
they will need in life.

They believe curricula should be geared
to competencies and economic usefulness.

They see knowledge as enabling learners
to be capable of earning their own way.

They encourage the practical application of learning.

They like hands-on activities and teaching technical skills.

They believe the best way is determined scientifically.

They use measured rewards.

As **leaders** they thrive on plans and timelines.

They tackle problems by making unilateral decisions.

They lead by personal forcefulness
and often inspire real quality.

They exercise authority with reward and punishment.
(Fewer good rules, but enforce them.)

They work hard to make their
organization productive and solvent.

They need staff who are task-oriented
and move quickly.

As **parents** they foster competence.

They try to give their children
the skills they will need in life.

They believe learning should
improve job skills and real-life skills.

They view knowledge as enabling their
children to become capable in finding
their own way.

They encourage their children to find
practical applications for what they learn.

They like active, hands-on family projects.

They believe success can be best judged
by whether or not something works.

They use measured rewards.

They see discipline as necessary to enable
children to eventually take their own power.

They tend to be inflexible and sometimes
lack the ability to express feelings.

STRENGTH: Practical application of ideas

FUNCTION BY: Gathering factual data from kinesthetic,
hands-on experience

GOALS: To align their view of the present with future security

FAVORITE QUESTION: How does this work?

TYPE FOUR: THE DYNAMIC LEARNER

As **learners** they perceive information concretely and process it actively.

They integrate experience and application.

They learn by trial and error.

They are believers in self-discovery.

They are very enthusiastic about newness.

They are adaptable, even relish change.

They excel when flexibility is needed.

They often reach accurate conclusions in the absence of logical justification.

They are risk-takers.

They are at ease with people.

They enrich reality by taking what is and adding to it.

Sometimes they are manipulative and pushy.

As **teachers** they are primarily interested in enabling learner self-discovery.

They try to help their students act on their visions.

They believe curricula should be geared to learners' interests.

They see knowledge as necessary for improving the larger society.

They engage in and encourage experiential learning.

They use a variety of instructional methods.

They are dramatic and seek to energize their students.

They attempt to create new forms, to stimulate new life, draw new boundaries.

They can be rash and manipulative.

As **leaders** they thrive on crisis and challenge.

They tackle problems by looking for patterns and scanning possibilities.

They lead by energizing people.

They exercise authority by holding up visions of what might be.

They work hard to enhance their organization's reputation as a front runner.

They need staff who can follow up and implement plans and details.

As **parents** they foster self-discovery.

They try to help their children have visions and act on them.

They believe learning should be geared to their child's interest.

They view knowledge as necessary for improving the larger society.

They encourage experiential learning for their children.

They like humorous and challenging (often competitive) family activities.

They are dramatic and entertaining.

They help their children seek new boundaries.

They see discipline as necessary to enable their children to become self-disciplined.

They tend to take on multiple activities, sometimes leading to inconsistencies and punishments that don't fit the crime.

STRENGTH: Action, getting things going

FUNCTION BY: Acting and testing experience

GOALS: To bring action to ideas

FAVORITE QUESTION: What if?

I desire that there be as many different persons
in the world as possible;
I would have each one be very careful
to find out and preserve
his own way.
— Henry David Thoreau

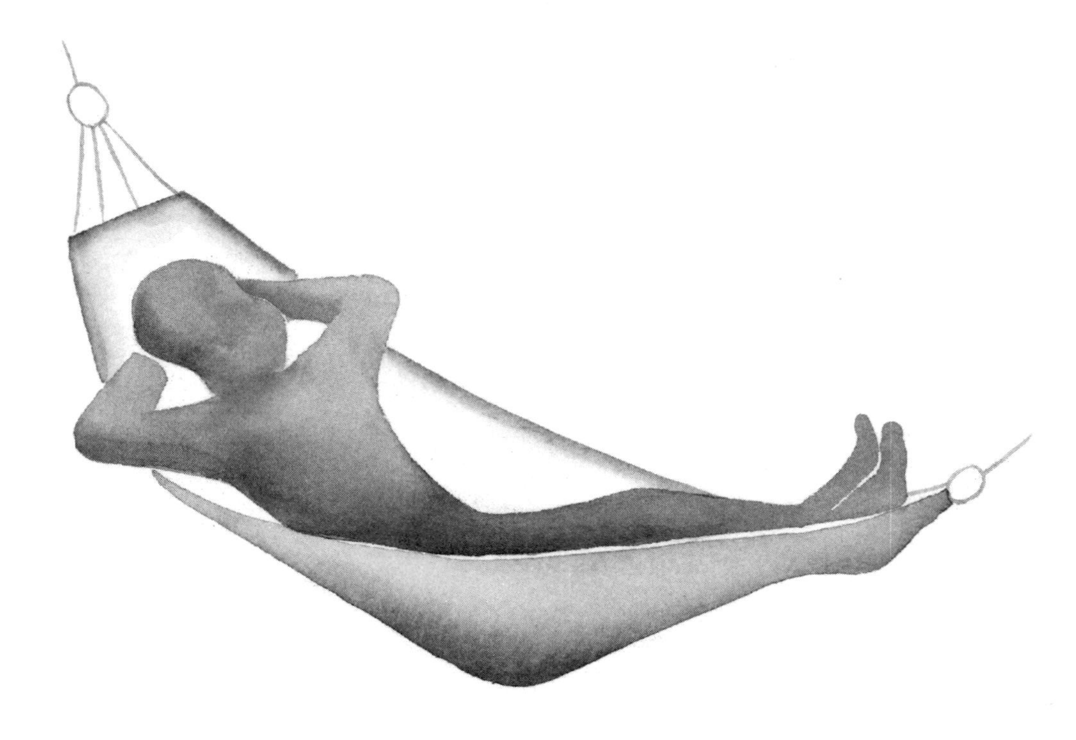

All four styles of learning
are equally valuable.

Each has its own strengths
and
weaknesses.

Whether you are a Type
One,
Two,
Three,
or
Four
or some combination of the above,
your style is how you learn.

It is your most graceful learning pattern.

It is a comfortable place for you to be
and you have every right to learn in that way.

Try to see it my way, only time will tell if
I am right or I am wrong.
While you see it your way,
there's a chance that we might fall apart before too long.
We can work it out. We can work it out.
— John Lennon and Paul McCartney

Combinations of Styles

When you take the Learning Type Measure (LTM)
to determine your learning style place,
a graphic image shows your strengths –
how much you go into your favored quadrant
as well as how much you function in the other three quadrants.

For example, while I am primarily a Type Four Learner,
I also have a very high Type Two Score.
I am intrigued by theory, especially if I can use it.

Rather than looking only at my Fourness,
you could understand my style better
if you knew my expertise in Quadrant Two
adds another dimension to my operative learning style.

A group of museum directors I worked with
scored as Type One and Type Two combinations.
They were reflective people,
interested in the cultures and the artifacts people create,
believers in the traditions of the past
as necessary for the present to understand itself.

A group of managers of a thriving, dynamic company
came out Type Three and Four combinations.
They were active, energetic people,
functioning in a fast-moving environment,
where decisions are made quickly.

Superintendents of school districts
also often come out as Types Three and Four.

Elementary school principals score as
combinations of Types One and Three,
an interesting phenomenon as these two types
tend to be antagonistic to one another.
The Ones focus on the people aspect of managing,
the Threes on the productivity and accountability aspect.
These are often in conflict.
When I query these principals,
they report that to be the case –
they often experience conflict in juggling
the human and productivity aspects of school management.

A group of physicists came out combinations
of Types Two and Three –
theorists who are interested in applicability.

Policemen come out primarily as Type Threes,
problem-solvers, as one would expect.
Yet many express their need for people skills,
for their work with wayward youth and in domestic difficulties,
both important aspects of police work.
These are qualities of Type One Learners,
not usually strong in the Threes.

The combinations learners form
as they move through the learning cycle
are important qualities of growth.
They are indicators of how well a person integrates
the different parts of the cycle.

So much energy
lies wrapped up in the shadow.
If we have exploited the ego
and worn out our known capacities,
our unused shadow
can give us a wonderful new lease on life.
— Jack Sanford

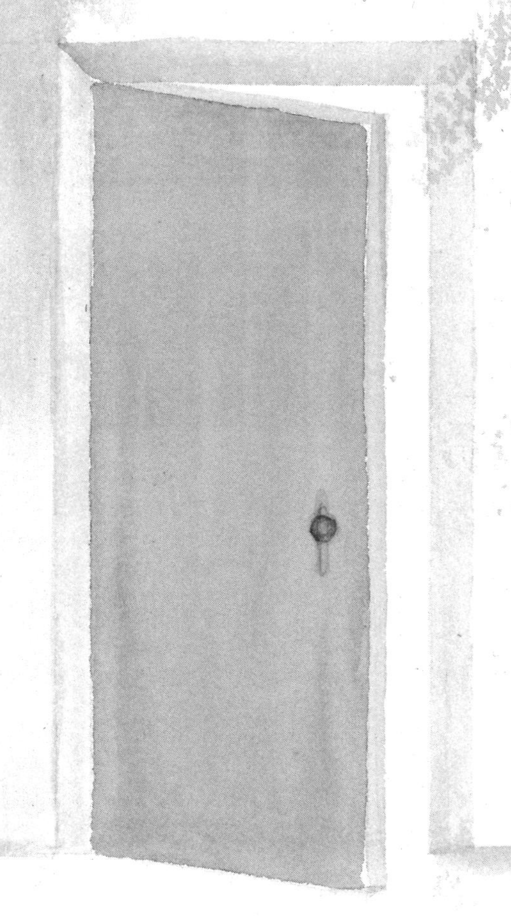

So it is important to examine
the quadrant in which you score the lowest –
your least developed place.

What ramifications does this have for your day-to-day
functioning at work, in school, in relationships?

Often it is your opposite quadrant
that scores the lowest,
that poses the most difficulty for you.
Generally, Ones have trouble with Quadrant Three skills
as Threes have trouble with Quadrant One skills.
And the same is true for Types Two and Four.

The challenge for the Ones is to learn to act more quickly,
to move to closure, to get the job done,
even while they understand the need
to give people the space to process at their own rates.

The challenge for the Threes is to learn to open themselves
to people, to honor the process time
people need to discover things for themselves,
even while they understand the need
to act, to move, to get the job done.

The challenge for the Twos is to learn to open themselves
to the ambiguity and unknown of the creative place,
even while they understand the need
for precision and the "right" data.

The challenge for the Fours is to learn to develop structure,
to go deeper, to avoid superficiality, to stay focused,
even while they understand the need
to cover a lot of territory in order to break boundaries,
to question, to push for renewal and growth.

Motion is the context of living.
We find meaning by and in our doing.
— Robert Kegan

Whatever your least developed quadrant is,
it is the place that can give you the most energy.
This is where you go to stretch,
to push out your boundaries,
to experience your own increase.

It is Jung's shadow side,
the place of the dark water
where the Beast lies waiting for Beowulf.
It is the courage challenge,
it is the dark side,
Mirkwood,
the white water.
It is the giver of energy.
It is new life.

If the cycle is the thing – if life moves us
from Oneness, to Twoness, to Threeness, to Fourness,
then growth comes from that motion,
from that rhythm around the cycle,
where we meet ourselves,
coming and going,
the comfortable and the uncomfortable.

We start in our perceptions,
move out of being caught in them –
separating ourselves,
coming to look at them as separate objects,
acting on our understandings,
refining them, editing them,
so we can return to ourselves,
more complete with our new subjectivities,
ready for new perceivings –
now a blend of our wisdom and the world's.

To the being fully alive,
the future is not ominous but a promise.
It surrounds the present as a halo.
— John Dewey

Styles are real
and quite pronounced in many of us.
It is reasonable that we operate
from our perceived strengths where we excel,
but real growth needs more.
Real growth needs the entire cycle.

As we move through life,
many of us eventually come
to conscious awareness of this cycle.
We search for meaning,
we recognize the importance of the big picture
and actively seek to understand it,
we struggle to apply what we learn to our daily lives,
and we often face the need for unique and creative solutions
to our problems.

We would be far better equipped
to find balance in our lives and our work
if we were introduced to this natural cycle early on,
if we were helped to understand its power –
if we could see the balance,
if it were made conscious for us.

To know a person,
look at the hopes and hoping that person is.
Not the hopes they have,
or the hoping they do,
but the hopes and hoping they are.
— Robert Kegan

The creation of energy
for growth and renewal
is found
in the stretchings,
not just in the lingerings.

Wholeness is challenge
as well as comfort.

It is a rhythm of letting go to rediscover,
of arriving back and understanding for the first time,
of finding oneself by going outside of oneself.

It is a frightening thing
to move from what is known to the unknown,
from the limits to the possibilities.
It is an act of hope.

To adapt for ourselves
what the world presents to us
is to construct our own lives.

It means we believe in our power to learn.
And learning is growth, is becoming.

CHAPTER THREE

About the Origins of the Cycle

A Learner's Story

Malcolm was in fourth grade and he did what he had to do. School was school and he accepted that. He did not find it exciting. He felt there were more interesting things to learn than what his teachers talked about. He got good grades and brought home fine report cards. He put in his time, but there was no real challenge for him. He did what he had to do and waited.

Intelligence develops
because it functions...
and it grows from within.
— Jean Piaget

Like a Greek dance,
the circle never closes.
No human mind
created the dance of learning,
invented its cycle.
Yet its rhythm of letting go to rediscover,
this meeting of ourselves coming and going,
has been described by researchers
in various ways
many times over.

Great minds
have reflected upon this cycle,
enriching the dance for each dancer.
In addition to Kurt Lewin and David Kolb,
I have chosen the following to include here
because their work resonates with my classroom experience:
Jean Piaget and Jerome Bruner,
Michael Polanyi and Alfred North Whitehead,
John Dewey and Robert Kegan.

Each of them
has contributed to my own
expanding understanding
of this natural learning cycle
as an ebbing and flowing cyclical pattern
that oftentimes moves in fits and starts.

Piaget's vision derives from
an open-systems evolutionary biology...
and places us in a single energy system
of all living things... with its primary attention
to an equilibrium in the world.
— Robert Kegan

Stop choosing
between chaos and order,
and live at the boundary between them,
where rest and action
move together.
— Rainer Maria Rilke

Jean Piaget, the great Swiss psychologist,
maintained that learning
is the result of learners'
interacting with the environment.
The learner experiences
and then connects those experiences
to what she already knows.

We feel, we take part, and we are taken in.
We compare the experience,
contrast it with what we already know.
We attach it or enfold it; it confirms.

Sometimes experiences shock us, take us back,
make us question our past knowing
or reveal facets that were unexplored,
or something suspended or ignored,
because we just couldn't handle it.

So we learn to balance the tension
between what is known and experienced
and the newness.

This calls us to do two things:
first, to continue to believe in our experience,
enriching and deepening our confirmed knowings,
and second, to open to new things,
even if these new things may confound
our previous knowings.

In order to grow
we must live in this tension;
we must keep this balance,
engage in this adaptive conversation,
both coming into ourselves
and going out to the world.

I am forever on the way.
— Maxine Greene

In addition to the in-and-out movement
between ourselves and the world,
we go through stages when we learn.

At first our knowing is tied
to what we can experience concretely.
We reach for things that interest us
and, in reaching for them, they exist for us.

Gradually we come to construct a world,
a world where things have their own properties apart from us.
We name them so they have a fit in our minds,
then we classify them
so we can order them and find order in them.

Finally we abstract them, generalize them,
come to understand that they are only examples of general things.
They can be considered apart
from our own specific concrete examples of them.

We conceptualize them.

A child feels the warmth and being of his grandmother
as she holds him, sings to him, feeds him.
Then he reaches for her, she exists for him concretely.

Then he comes to name her "Grandmother"–
she has a designation, a word, a symbol.
Finally he comes to realize
that "grandmotherness" exists in the world.
The child abstracts from his grandmother
the qualities that fit–*for him*–all the world's grandmothers.

He comes to an understanding of grandmotherness.

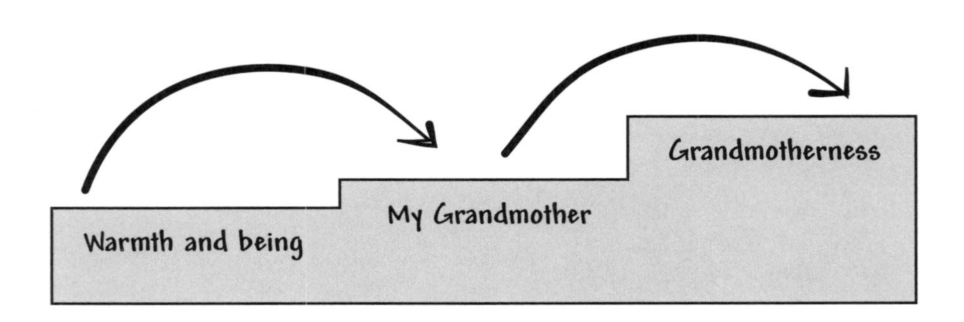

Each of these three modes of representation
has its unique way . . .
each places a powerful impress
on the mental life of human beings
at different ages
and their interplay persists
as one of the major features
of adult intellectual life.
—Jerome Bruner

Bruner, building on Piaget, looked at how
humans represent what they experience –
how they see it and hold it in their mind's eye.

He looked at the developing stages,
how infants grasped things,
how they mouthed things.
how they experienced things by acting on them.
Things were lived with rather than thought.
This was the first stage of learning something.

Then, he noted, children came to be able
to hold pictures of things in their minds,
even when they were separated from them,
even when they were not acting on them.

They could represent with pictures
images of the things rather than the things themselves.
This was the second stage of intellectual growth.

Finally the children discovered things had names.
(They even named some things themselves.)

Picture the young Helen Keller discovering wordness:
"water" symbolizing the coolness, the liquidness
running through her fingers
as Annie Sullivan wildly pumped the well handle.

From hands, to images, to words.

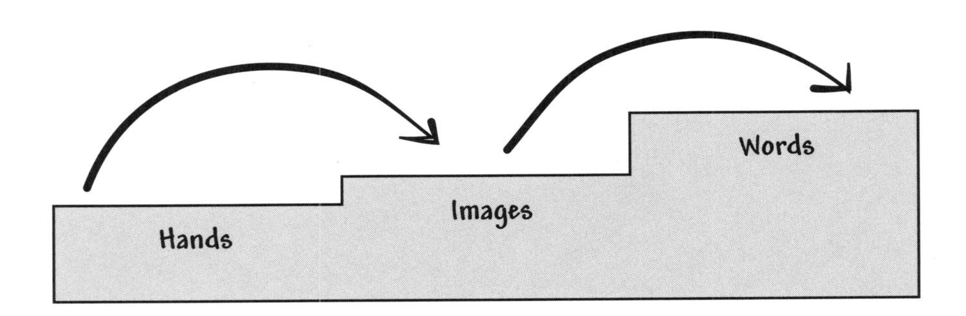

We must know where the gold lies
within ourselves.
— David Whyte

This naming was the third stage.
This naming led to structures
that were imposed on the perceived world.

The need for structures often results in a loss of wholeness
because parts are singled out for naming.
We sacrifice knowing at its whole, round level
for the sake of making order out of things.

In the nature of naming lies
the danger that the ineffable mystery of things will be lost
or in time forgotten entirely.

The child who comes to understand grandmotherness
has achieved a conceptual wholeness,
who, what, how grandmothers are;
he can generalize the idea.
It is a wholeness, a wholeness of the mind.
But there is also another wholeness,
a wholeness of being,
the warmth and uniqueness of his own grandmother,
whence the abstraction came.

To replace the real with an abstraction of the real,
and to make that abstraction the primary thing,
is to deny that real life is the final test.
To really know, we must do both.

We also must remember that the stages of growth
are not the only movement in human development.
They are the manifestations of principles
that govern growth, but they are only a part
of the story of how humans develop,
of how they travel around the cycle.

... thinking is not only intentional,
it is also necessarily fraught
with the roots that it embodies.
It has a from-to structure.
— Michael Polanyi

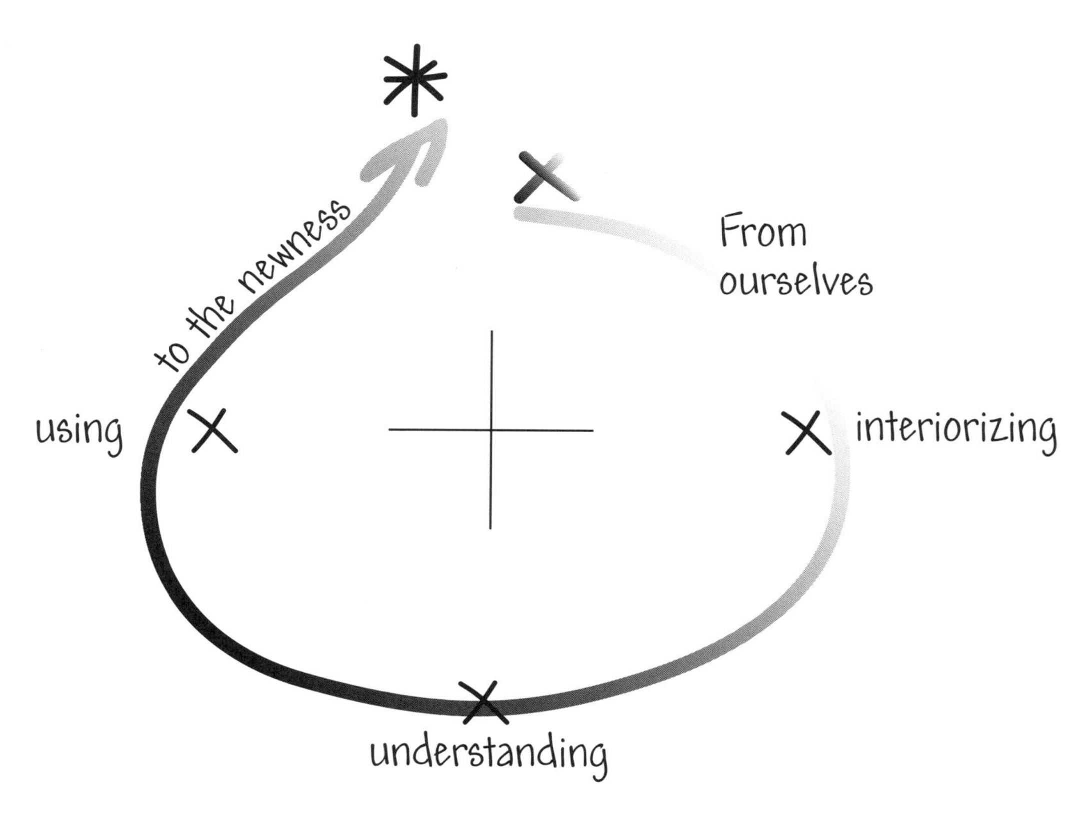

Michael Polanyi emphasized the beginning
of the learning cycle.

We are what we know.
All learning begins with us,
and it depends on where we come from.
It depends on who we are at that moment.

The knowing that is us at any given moment
is the composite of the things we understand,
much of which we never openly express.

We always go from ourselves to the newness,
and we know more than we can tell.

If we are successful in experiencing
and understanding
and using the new learning,
it will become a part of us.

If we interiorize it,
(feel how we feel about it),
attend to it, intend to know it,
our motivation moves us
to understanding
and to the **use** of that understanding,
which is the real learning.
We bring it home.

The cycle repeats.

An education that does not begin
by evoking initiative
and end by encouraging it
must be wrong.
— Alfred North Whitehead

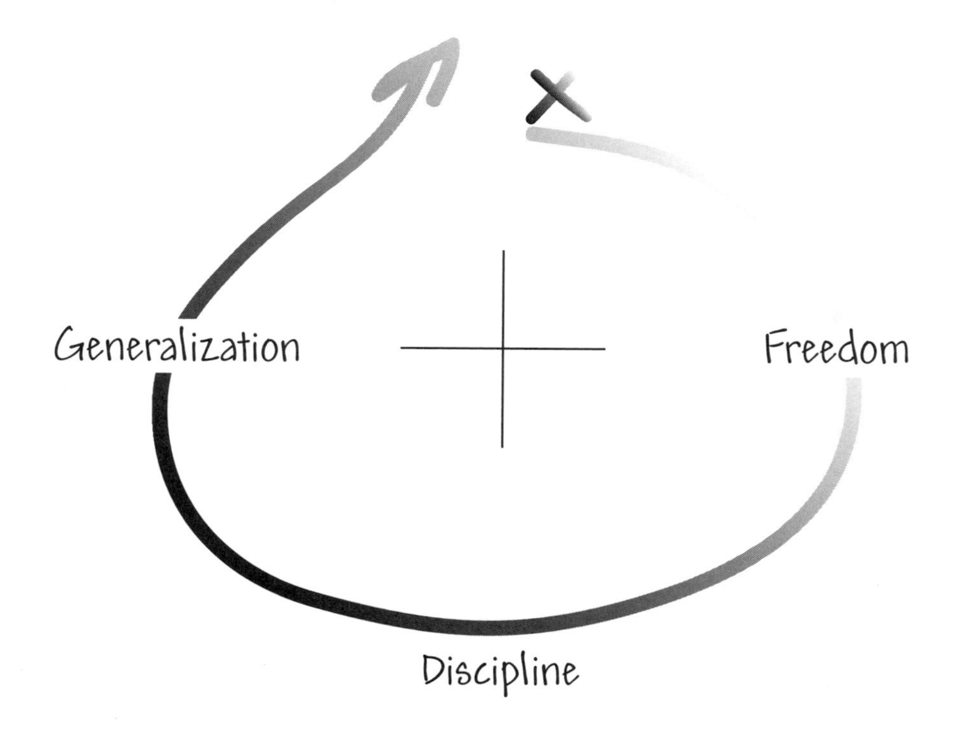

Alfred North Whitehead also described a cycle;
he called it three "periods" in education.

The first he called the **freedom** stage,
the place where the student must choose to be interested,
must move toward self-development through joy,
a process of becoming,
of noticing what happens,
wondering,
and then being filled with wonder.
The emphasis here is on freedom,
freedom that allows the learner to see,
to make independent choices.

The second period he called the **discipline** stage,
a necessary period of development of best practice,
examining the data, learning the facts,
concentrating with purpose.
The third he called **generalization**,
where something definite is known,
where general rules and laws are apprehended,
when the learner is ready to shed the details
in favor of the active application of the principles.

Here real learning happens because
knowledge has become invested with possibilities;
learning has become active wisdom,
"connecting a zest of life to knowledge."

The cycle repeats.

When intellectual experience
and its material
are taken to be primary
the cord that binds nature and experience is cut.
— John Dewey

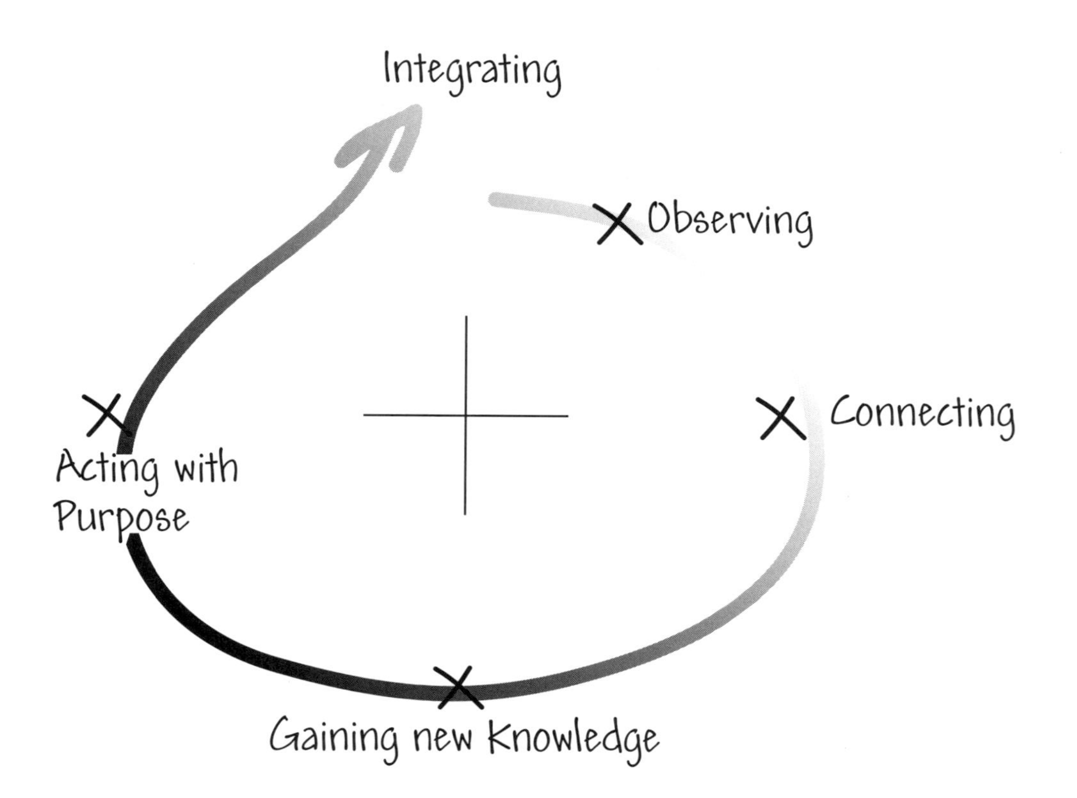

John Dewey maintained
that, if learning is real,
it creates purpose and direction
leading to change
and then on to transformation.

He illustrated with a cycle.

Observing,
then connecting what we experience to the past,
then gaining new knowledge,
(and judging that knowledge
in relation to what we already know),
then acting with purpose,
finally integrating new learning into our lives.

The cycle repeats.

The cistern contains,
the fountain overflows.
— William Blake

Oftentimes
educators and researchers,
while understanding these movements as stages,
(one a lower form of knowing,
another a step up, a third higher and so on),
make the serious error
of believing that when we abstract,
when we can conceive things apart from their concrete reality,
we reach the ultimate step on the thinking ladder,
that to return to the real is somehow a step down.

It is the real that informs, enlightens, and renews our abstractions,
over and over again. They cannot be separated.
Yet in schoolrooms and work places everywhere
the separation goes on.
We teach botany without flowers,
astronomy without the stars,
geology without the earth,
mathematics without real problems.
No wonder learners do not understand.

This is failure to understand the movement of being,
the motion of humanness,
the development of knowing,
motion because our knowing is accomplished
by what we **do in the world**,
what Kegan calls "our evolutionary activity."
How we feel and think
and think about our feelings
and feel about our thoughts
and act on those feelings and thoughts
and feel anew.

The cycle goes hand in hand with the stages.
It is how we make meaning in our lives.

Each naming requires a new naming.
— Paulo Freire

These movements –
the ways we are in the world repeat,
deepening, we hope, as we go:
from feeling
to reflecting,
to symbolizing,
to acting,
to creating new feeling.

If we stay in tune with this "movement of meaning" (Kegan),
our understandings of things
never become the only understanding.
The conversation goes on.
The possibility of newness always exists.
Reality needs continual revisiting, revising.

There is such a danger in naming
especially when we believe
that if we understand things conceptually
we have reached **the** high point in thinking.
Things can become bound by our conceptions of them.
The name can become the thing.

In the introduction to Sherwood Anderson's *Winesburg, Ohio,*
"The Book of the Grotesques,"
an old carpenter walks the road of life in a writer's dream.
All about him are piles of truths,
hundreds of them.
The writer sees all the people
he has known in his life
snatching up the truths,
some dozens of them.
And the more they grab,
the more grotesque they become.
And the old carpenter, because he came
"the nearest thing to what is understandable and loveable
of all the grotesques in the book,"
is the least twisted as he passes by on the road of life.

Perfect truth
is possible only with knowledge,
and in knowledge
the whole essence of the thing
operates on the soul
and is joined essentially to it.
— Benedict Spinoza

Humans go from the simultaneous experience
of things in their wholeness,
from feeling them, imaging them,
to symbols of them, names of them,
(even naming them themselves).

We must not stop with the naming –
we need to go back to ever new experiences,
back to being with them and in them
in new ways
because we know more,
because we understand more,
because we have gone around the cycle.

We lose so much
if we don't pay attention to this process.

No matter how elegant and true the symbols,
they can never replace the real things.
The symbolic and the real must be held together.
We must know
and be open to what we do not know
at the same time.

When we understand
the abstraction of "Grandmotherness"
as well as our own grandmothers,
we fold back around in a circle –
a circle that leads to deeper knowing,
where the real
and the concept of the real
exist simultaneously.

As we develop our ability to know,
we are experiencing at the same time.
We are knowing **and** being.

One must learn to think well
before learning to think;
afterwards it proves too difficult.
— Anatole France

It is human that we grow through the cycle differently.
Each of these ways of relating to things –
by acting on them,
by picturing them,
or by creating symbols for them
(with words or numbers),
and then acting on them anew –
has its own unique way of being in experience.

The trick is to remember to pay attention to
and to honor them all
and most of all to return to the cycle,
to revisit the real
even as our ability to abstract the real
becomes refined and polished.

It is precisely because we have become such
refined and polished conceptualizers
that we need to return to the real
the more often.

My identity has to be perceived as multiple
even as I strive towards
some inherent notion
of what is humane and decent and just.
— Maxine Greene

Learning,
while admittedly progressing like steps on a ladder,
also cycles or even spirals...
ebbs and flows,
and moves in fits and starts
into our adult lives in many idiosyncratic, adapted forms.

What if my sensorimotor stage as an infant,
where I reach and grasp for things,
develops into a bodily kinesthetic preference
that continues to operate throughout my life,
enhancing my ability to know through my body...

What if my imaging stage
develops into a visual knowing
that remains a strong approach to conceptualizing
throughout my life
contributing to my ability to really see...

What if my symbolizing
becomes a primary focus
always coloring my feeling, reflecting,
thinking and doing...

Or what if they are parallel,
running through their developmental phases
side-by-side,
all dependent upon the circumstances and contexts
of individual learners...

Or what if they can function simultaneously –
the way a calliope plays
with the pipes up and down
at differing heights,
at different times,
coloring a certain time and space
with different tones and shades of sound...

... this activity,
this adaptive conversation,
is the very source of,
and the unifying context for,
thought and feeling...

it is about knowing and being.
— Robert Kegan

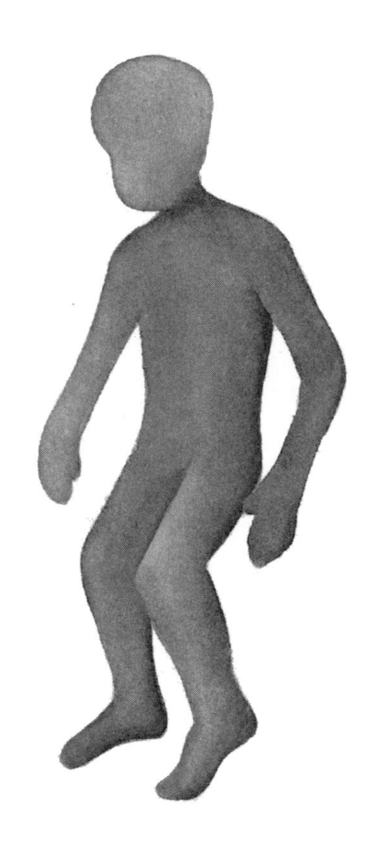

I believe all of this is true.
I believe these stages exist and operate
as a series of steps,
also in parallel dimensions,
and sometimes simultaneously
in a self-renewing cycle.

We grasp the concrete,
we make images,
we classify,
we generalize,
we use,
we grasp anew.

I originally approached learning styles
believing style was the key
to student learning style differences.

Now I believe the cycle is at the heart of these differences,
and style is merely
the personal manifestation
of the unique ways
each of us travels the cycle.

It is the cycle we must understand.

All depends upon a breaking free,
a leap, and then a question.
I would like to claim
that this is how learning happens
and that the educative task
is to create situations
in which the young are moved
to begin to ask, in all the tones of voice there are,
Why?
— Maxine Greene

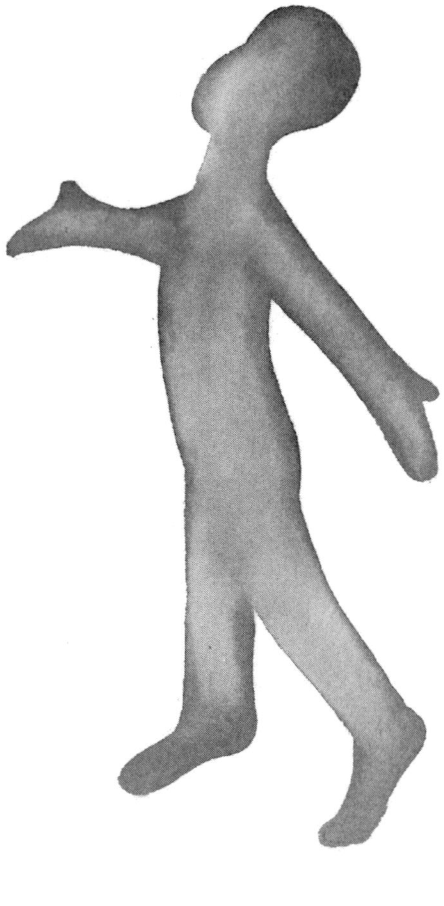

Researchers made the cycle more conscious,
drew out its implications,
realized it included many more learners.

A model suggested itself to me,
a model that flowed from the direct knowledge
of the natural cycle that I had used in my teaching.

The model I created and call
The 4MAT System®
makes the place of different learning styles
explicit within this natural cycle.

To understand this natural learning model,
we must first look more deeply
into how the brain creates a mind.
We must specifically examine what has come to be called
right- and left-mode preferences in learning
and how people differ in this regard
both in school
and on the job.

We need to understand
what right- and left-mode processing is,
how people differ in their ability to use both,
and how these hemisphere-mode-processing preferences
fit on the cycle.

CHAPTER FOUR

About Learning and the Brain: Right- and Left-Mode Processing and Style

A Learner's Story

Jimmy was in second grade, and he did not like to read. That made school difficult, as his teachers asked him to do a lot of reading. He enjoyed it immensely, though, when others read to him. His younger brother, a first-grader, used to read him stories every night. And he would say, "Read me another one, Dave."

He excelled in math and art. He loved to work alone on projects. He never wanted help. When he was asked to create illustrations for a story or build something to depict a math concept, he was totally turned on. His mother would put him to bed only to see the light on under his door hours later. She would go in and there he would be. "Mom, I'm working on a project and I just dreamed how it should be."

He had a rigid second grade teacher. He called her the "Mean Screamer." Her time was always different from his time. He was either finished too fast or he took too long, because when he got really interested in a project, he was a perfectionist. Once his teacher actually said to him in exasperation, "I didn't say you had to do your best work, Jimmy, just get it done!"

He kept school glue, Popsicle sticks, pipe cleaners, shoe boxes and old toy creatures under his bed in the hopes he would be asked to make something new. He was happiest when he had a problem he could solve by creating a three-dimensional solution. His problem with reading continued until late into third grade. But he never allowed it to put him down; he was simply too busy doing other kinds of things.

To see,
to perceive
is more than to recognize.
—John Dewey

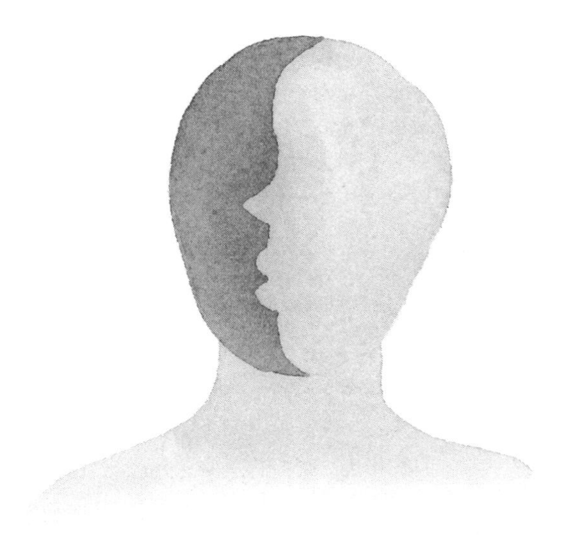

No discussion of learning is complete
without examining
some of the specifics of
how the brain creates a mind.

Current brain studies,
specifically right- and left-mode processing research,
are adding much to our understanding
of the natural cycle and style.

Educators who seek to understand differences
in the ways students approach learning
would do well to ponder the significance
of these split-brain studies.
Understanding right- and left-mode characteristics
and the strategies and techniques used to engage them
can have a profound effect on student success.

But we need to be very clear
about what they are and what they are not.

... reflecting on
our own direct involvement
in the area of hemispheric specialization for many years,
we have become increasingly aware of the "dichotomania" problem.
[Author's note: *Dichotomania* refers to a tendency of the theorist
to exaggerate the role of right versus left into two totally separate parts.]

... At the same time,
we have become even more impressed
with the reality of hemispheric differences
and with their potential
for helping us understand
the brain mechanisms
underlying higher mental functions.
— Sally Springer and Georg Deutsch

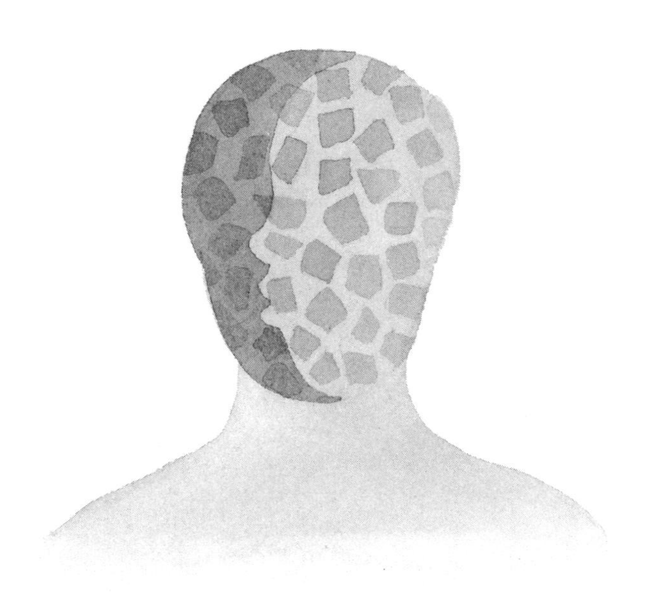

The two sides of the human cerebral cortex function differently.
They are two different mental operations
with separate modes of consciousness.
Normally each side works in cooperation with the other
and complements the other.

The Left Mode:

- Operates with analysis, examines cause and effect.
- Breaks things down into parts,
  examines and categorizes.
- Seeks and uses language and symbols.
  (The English alphabet promotes and reinforces
  left-mode strategies.)
- Abstracts experience for comprehension, generates theory, creates models.
- Is sequential, works in time.

Analysis
Parts
Categories
Cause and effect
Linearity
Grids
Sequence
Reason
Objectivity

Left mode knows those things we can describe with precision,
classifying, discriminating, naming.

We do, in fact, have two hemispheres,
and we cannot get away from that fact.
Each hemisphere does operate
somewhat differently
from the other,
and we cannot get away from the tangles
that difference proposes.
— Gregory Bateson

The Right Mode:

- Operates out of being, intuits feeling states.
  (Things perceived are often indescribable.)
- Sees wholes, forms images, mental combinations.
- Seeks and uses patterns, relationships, connections.
- Functions visuo-spatially –
  manipulation of form, distance and space.
- Is simultaneous.

Apprehension
Wholes
Images
Patterns
Relationships
Connections
Simultaneity
Heart
Subjectivity

Right mode knows more than it can tell,
filling gaps, thinking aside, imaging.

The general thrust of the neuroscience implications
is to open education to the possibilities
of a greater range
of human mental, intellectual
and learning capabilities.
— Paul Messier, US Department of Education

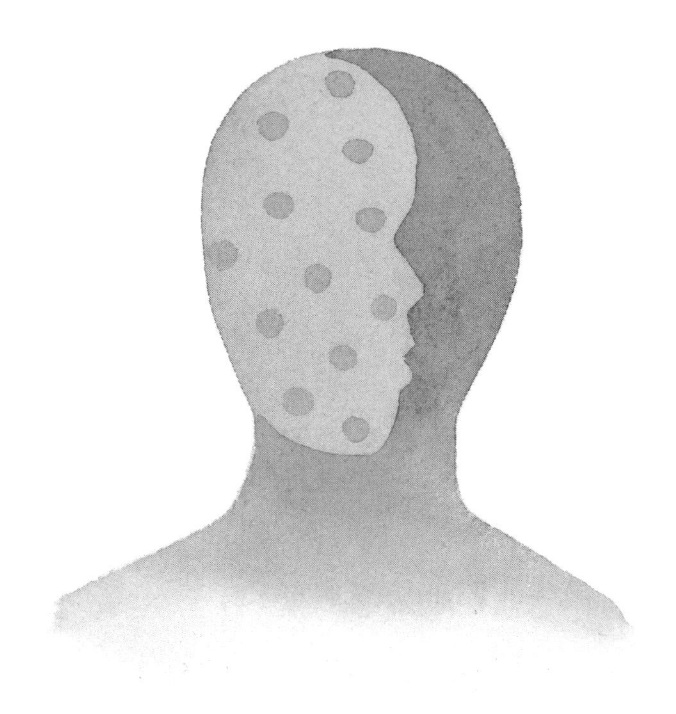

The Left Mode is linear.
The Right Mode is round.

The Left Mode thinking skills are of high order:
language, analysis, sequence, logic and objectivity.

The Right Mode's roundness
is thinking of the highest order as well.

It is multi-faceted.
It moves, it clears space.
It sees the partially eclipsed,
flourishing on gaps.
It creates connections.
It problem-solves sideways, obliquely,
flanking, circling, cantering,
long underground, then all-at-once.

The cognitive processes used for language
and for spatial-perceptual functions
are incompatible
and therefore had to develop in separate brain areas.
. . . the left and right modes of processing
would mutually interfere
if they existed within the same hemisphere.
— Jerry Levy

Linear is:

a great manuscript,
the perfect golf lesson,
the straight arrow,
finishing with time left over.

A skilled actuary,
a great diagram,
the correct directions,
understanding incrementally,
when you finally categorize all the parts.

Staying on task,
hearing exactly what is said,
thinking carefully before acting,
when the statistics match.

The edges,
time,
multiple pieces,
Hm-mm.

The perfect sequence,
analyzing the zone,
the grids,
the nouns.

The whole,
though it be long,
stands almost complete and finished in my mind,
so that I can survey it at a glance.
Nor do I hear in my imagination
the parts successively,
but I hear them, as it were,
all at once.
What delight this is I cannot tell!
— Wolfgang Amadeus Mozart

Round is:

a great storyteller,
the perfect golf shot,
a consummate musical moment,
the instant in slow motion.

A skilled sailor,
a great performance,
the perfect sentence,
knowing instantly that something is true,
when you finally understand how the parts fit.

Doing more than one thing at a time,
hearing what people don't say,
choosing skillfully when there is no time to think,
when you suddenly know you're in deep trouble.

The essence,
timelessness,
oneness,
ah-ha.

Street sense,
being in the zone,
networks,
all the verb things that you can add "ing" to.

Scholars and artists
both work from knowledge.
Scholars get theirs with conscientious thoroughness
along projected lines of logic.
Poets theirs cavalierly…
they stick to nothing deliberately
but let what will
stick to them like burrs
where they walk in the fields.
— Robert Frost

Speech is linear, left,
one word, one thought, following the other,
in structured, sequential order.

Some learners who are really at ease in round thinking
have trouble articulating their thinking.
They must be linear to speak their thinking,
so the imagery of poetry suits them better
where words round into holograms
and metaphors weave connections.
They often use their hands as they struggle,
making sculptures in the air
as they try to articulate what words cannot.
Speech sometimes defeats them.
It is not compatible with the way they know.
They know much more than they can tell.

Other learners are at ease with the linear.
They can describe precisely what they mean.
They are frustrated by ambiguity and roundness.
They are not at ease when they cannot specify.

Both kinds of thinkers need to enhance the gift of language,
round thinkers by stretching toward precision and clarity,
linear thinkers by embracing nuance and connotation.

Both kinds of thinkers need to be honored
for being who they are
and what they bring.

The inspired moment
may sometimes be described
as a kind of hallucinatory state of mind:
one half of the personality emotes and dictates
while the other half listens and notates.
The half that listens had better look the other way,
had better simulate a half attention only,
for the half that dictates is easily disgruntled
and avenges itself for too close inspection
by fading entirely away.
— Aaron Copland

All excellence is both.

Listen while the master storyteller
integrates the language skills of the Left Mode
with the imaging skills of the Right.
She takes the linearity of speech
and weaves roundness
with pictures, intonations, dialogues, colors.

Attend the poet who chooses words
with the most careful precision
and forms crystal moments
where events hang forever suspended
as living holograms.

Be with the composer who hears the whole,
then in painstaking sequence
creates the notations
which create the linearity
for the musicians to follow
in order to create the round he hears.

Rose Merrill, while a Senior at Walnut Hill School,
in Natick, Massachusetts,
wrote the following anthem to both.

Ambidextrous

With my hands, I sculpt…

My left and right
are opposites:
yin and yang,
moon and sun,
woman and man,
creative and logical.
They are two separate forces
connected by wrist, arm, shoulder,
to my reconciling body.

One cold, spring morning
when I was eight,
I noticed
how my right hand carried the burden
of my heavy school bag
while my left swung freely at my side.
I thought, “It isn’t fair
that my right hand does all the work.”
That hand threaded needles,
wrote tests,
washed dishes,
did cartwheels,
and wiped my bum…
yet here was the left hand
off in her own world:
she picked dandelions,
wore plastic rings and bracelets,
waved from car windows,
and, at times, she would put
a paintbrush to paper
and an entire world might emerge
from beneath the bristles.

Her frivolity was hardly fair…

I didn't realize my left hand toiled as well,
weaving my history into memories.
I didn't know then
that she was collecting the
images, smells, sensations
that would someday become art...

But, years later,
when the left triumphed in the studio,
the victory was empty...

I need the logic of my right hand
for the precision of mathematics,
the intricacy of structure,
blueprints that do not limit;
rather, they allow.
If, like an architect, you have the basic plan –
a house with bedrooms,
bathrooms, kitchen –
you can move beyond.

You can add on an observation tower,
stained glass, or a labyrinth.
The left will always have the visions.

This was my metamorphosis:
as a butterfly emerging from its chrysalis,
so I grasp my paintbrush in one hand,
my protractor in the other.
It was you who brought my hands close,
all of you, my teachers.

You took both
left and right and led me,
ambidextrous now,
(like a child learning to walk)

to the horizon where these opposing lines
can touch and merge.

Carl Orff, Choirmaster of the Vienna Boys Choir,
would not accept a child into his choir
who had already learned to read and write.

Mozart asked his wife
to read stories to him while he composed.
By distracting his left brain
with spoken language, his music-oriented right brain
was freer to compose unimpeded.

To learn to do both is to be patient.

Spoken language, silent or aloud,
if applied too soon,
interferes with round thinking,
prevents it from running its course,
from getting where it needs to go.

The right mode,
in order to do its thing,
functions (in the main) without words,
using pictures,
discerning the affect, the feeling things,
creating metaphors,
picking up tones and emotional colors,
synthesizing.

Words need to wait,
the naming comes after,
after the mullings, the ruminating and the mutterings.

I do not so easily think in words...
after being hard at work having arrived at results
that are perfectly clear...
I have to translate my thoughts in a language
that does not run evenly with them.
— Francis Galton, Geneticist

If children are pressured
for language too soon,
it may actually interfere
with their right mode development.

And when adults come to language too soon,
it may interfere with their creativity.

Fluency in one mode
may hamper fluency in the other.

(If people name and classify others
with permanent labels,
they never come to know them.)

The translation from perception to language
is oftentimes difficult if not impossible.

Many inventive people
have difficulty with this translation.

... there is often complex interaction
between the two hemispheres
in any given task.
In general, one might say
that the left thinks in words and numbers,
while the right thinks visually,
in pictures and images in three-dimensional space.
— Thomas West

Leonardo and Michelangelo were lefties.

Thomas West describes
the learning difficulties experienced
by many of the great minds of this and past centuries.

Undoubtedly these were not difficulties at all,
but a keen gift of a different kind.

Michael Faraday,
who laid the foundation for classical field theory –
had early problems with speech,
was deficient in spelling, punctuation, and capitalization,
had what he considered an unreliable memory.
"I was never able to make a fact my own without seeing it."

James Clerk Maxwell,
who developed the theory of the electromagnetic field –
was awkward and hesitant in speech throughout his life,
relied heavily on geometric approaches to ideas.
The visual-spatial dominated his work.

Albert Einstein,
who developed the theory of relativity –
had a poor memory for words and texts,
tended toward disorganization,
and had unusual difficulty with spelling.

Lewis Carroll,
English writer and mathematician –
had difficulty remembering dates,
was a life-long stutterer.

Henri Poincare,
extraordinary mathematical thinker –
talked very badly at first – he thought more rapidly than
he could speak,
had a marked propensity to doodle,
measured as imbecile on the Binet test of IQ,
had a powerful visual-spatial memory.

In some cases, it seems that
the greater the fluency with nonverbal thought,
the greater the dysfluency of verbal communication.
This tendency might create difficulties
for those in universities and other institutions
where verbal proficiency is seen
as a major indicator of intellectual competence.

Perhaps if there were a greater awareness
of this paradoxical tendency,
we could begin to look past verbal dysfluency –
or even fluency – to measure the true value
of the ideas that lie behind.
Perhaps more important still,
we might also learn to see
some of the real power of nonverbal modes of thought,
however difficult they may be to communicate in words.
— Thomas West

Thomas Alva Edison,
American inventor –
had difficulty with spelling and grammar,
had high mechanical and visualization skills,
exhibited high use of metaphor to manipulate ideas and transform images.
His particular way of reading involved a lot of skipping and skimming.
"My father thought I was stupid, and
I almost decided I must be a dunce."

Like Einstein and Edison and other great thinkers,
many people create pictures in their minds.
They convert ideas into images.
This talent has great significance.
The ability to generate, overlay, juxtapose and transform images
is a precise mental mechanism
as "elegant as the internal schema that form the foundations of language." (Cooper and Shepherd)

Yet researchers maintain that powerful visual imagination
seems to come sometimes at a cost.

West describes this phenomenon:
[But they sometimes are] "so much in touch with
their visual-spatial, nonverbal, right-hemisphere modes of thought
that they have had difficulty in doing
orderly, sequential, verbal-mathematical, left-hemisphere tasks
in a culture where left-hemisphere capabilities are so highly valued."

The need for better methods
by which to detect, measure,
and develop the nonverbal
components of intellect is
becoming widely recognized.
— Joseph Bogen

So the critical question
is not are children right- or left-brained,
but are their environments equipping them
to use both hemispheres interactively.
— Jane Healy

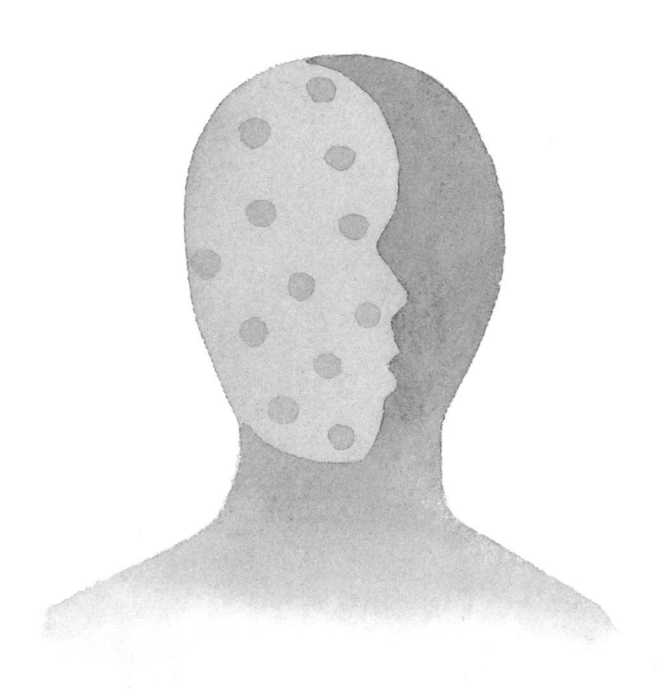

Because people are measured against a left-mode standard,
right-mode learners are judged inadequate.

How many slip through the cracks,
believing themselves incapable of school-type learning?

Believe me when I tell you they are legion.
They are in my audiences in large numbers.
They dread the thought of any type of schooling even as adults.

It's a double bind.
It isn't only that they are not getting what they need to learn their way;
it's that they are not getting what they need to learn either way.
They are so turned off by the ubiquitous left-mode teaching
they find everywhere, they turn away from it,
and the irony is they need it.

And the left-mode learners who succeed in school
become elitist about precision and logic
and turn away from the round, flowing patterning they need
to move into the genius of the right.

Excellence and higher-order thinking demand
that we use both modes of processing.
We need to honor both sides of the brain.

We persist in talking-head type lectures,
and logical, sequential problem-solving models,
when we also need to teach interactively as well,
with hands-on, real-life, messy, round problem solving.

Left-mode learners come to believe
that only reason and logic are to be trusted,
robbing them of creative excellence.

And right-mode learners come to believe that the way they approach
learning is inferior and not be be trusted,
robbing them of the belief in their ability to learn at all.

Enriching experiences early in life
lead to permanent brain changes
that enhance problem-solving capabilities.

We can enrich heredity
through enriching the environment...

giving us optimism about the potential for growth in the brain,
and warnings about the effects of impoverishment.
— Marian Cleeves Diamond

Can we influence the propensities people have
for the skillful use of their brains?
Can we intervene in the downward spiral right-mode learners
find themselves in?

Marian Cleeves Diamond thinks so.
In her book *Enriching Heredity* she maintains
it is critical to the continued health
of the nerve cells in our brains
that we use them.
Passive observation is not enough.
We must interact with our world.

Every part of the nerve cell alters its dimensions
in response to the environment.
Decreasing stimulation diminishes it,
increasing stimulation enlarges it.

At every age studied –
birth, babyhood, young adulthood, old age –
both the enriched environment
and the impoverished environment
showed anatomical effect.

One of the most important outcomes of the cerebral laterality research is the increased insight and appreciation for the importance of nonverbal forms of learning, intellect and communication.
— Roger Sperry

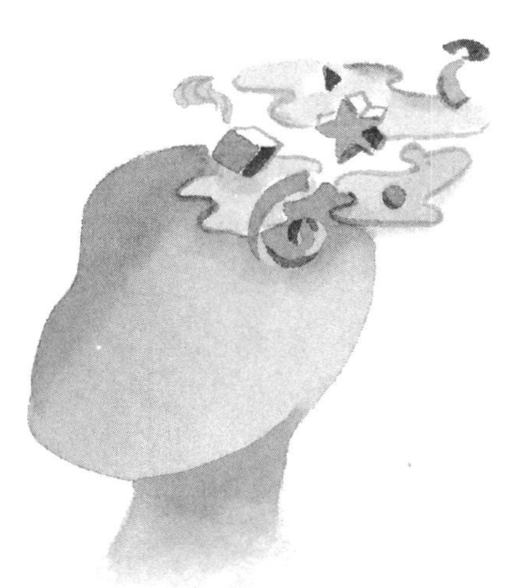

The expectations people have for us
and the tasks people set for us
affect **how** we learn.
The more we are asked to do left-mode tasks,
the more we learn to learn in only that way
and the more right-mode learners are marginalized.

The demands of the tasks may nudge the brain
into one mode over the other.

Traditional schooling trains the left mode
often to the detriment of the right.
The strategies that take place in our classrooms
focus primarily on left-mode thinking.

This is simply not an acceptable model of instruction.

But it is not just schools that are at fault.
Traditional companies reward left-mode processing
often to the detriment of the right.
The strategies that run our businesses
focus primarily on left-mode thinking and left-mode skills.

If neuropsychologists are right
(and the research is deafening)
that these two processes, while separate and unique,
are inextricably linked –
imagine what that means.

In prayer, in the creative process,
these two parts of ourselves,
the mind and the heart,
the intellect and the intuition,
the conscious and the subconscious mind,
stop fighting each other
and collaborate.
— Madeleine L'Engle

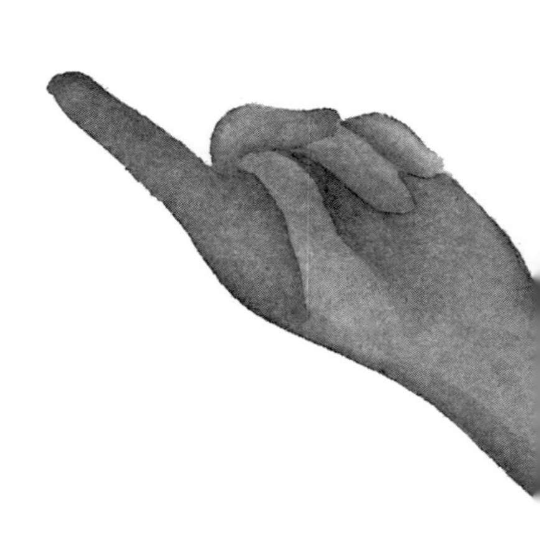

Human brains continually blend
analysis and synthesis,
although different individuals tend to favor
one mode over the other.

How we structure tasks,
set expectations,
stimulate or impoverish the environment,
and most of all honor these differences
creates the balance
or imbalance in learners.

If we continue to focus on only one mode of processing,
we do great harm to the whole brain.

If we incorporate round, nonverbal thinking
into learning and working
and honor its manifestations equally
with analytic acuity –
creative excellence has a thriving chance,
enhancing the powers of
choice,
discovery,
and promise.

All learners will then have the opportunity
to become.

Reason sets the boundaries far too narrowly for us,
and would have us accept only the known –
and that too with limitations –
and live in a known framework,
just as if we were sure how far life actually extends.
As a matter of fact,
day after day we live far beyond the bounds of consciousness;
without our knowledge,
the life of the unconscious is also going on within us.
The more the critical reason dominates,
the more impoverished life becomes;
but the more of the unconscious,
and the more of myth we are capable of making conscious,
the more of life we integrate.
Overvalued reason has this in common with political absolutism:
under its dominion the individual is pauperized.
— Carl Jung

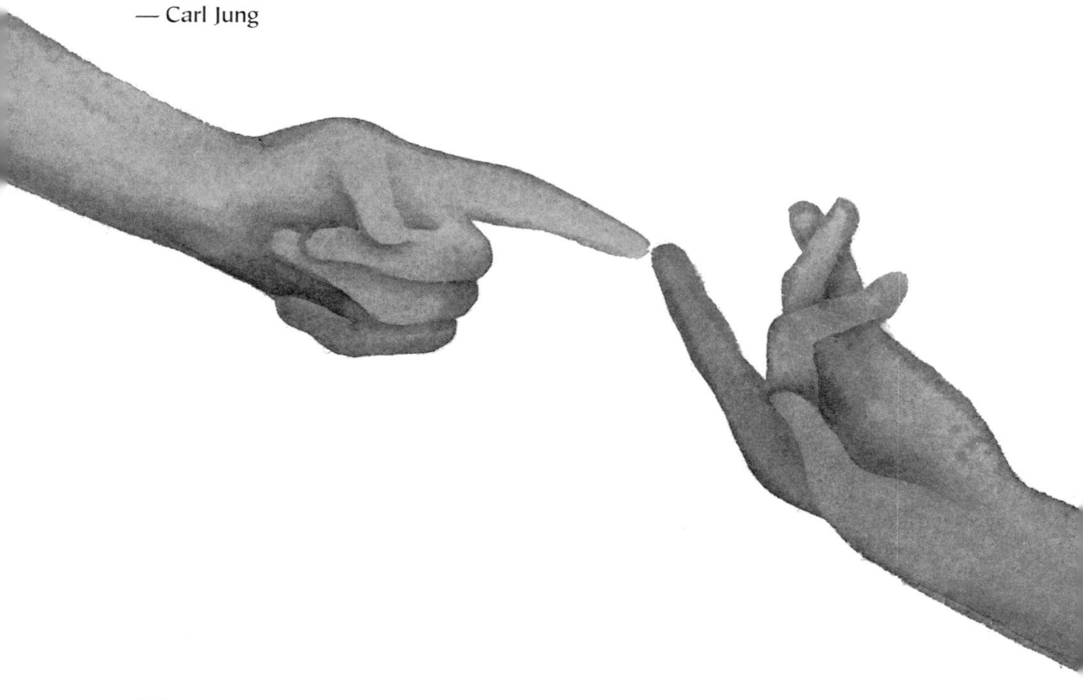

What kind of excellence is possible
if we deny
or are ashamed to acknowledge
or even label as inferior (as some researchers have done)
a major processing mode of humanness –
the round, random, ranging, relating right mode?

What kind of excellence is possible
if we acknowledge, honor,
and even celebrate both modes of human processing
and design our instruction and our work tasks accordingly?

Clearly we must do both.

CHAPTER FIVE

About Balanced Learning: The 4MAT Cycle

A Learner's Story

Mario thought school was great. His favorite classes were those where he could talk and talk. He doesn't remember much about the content of school, although he did very well and went on to college and a successful career. But what he does remember is all his classmates and all his teachers, all the way even through high school. The study groups, the ideas shared, the give and take of discussion and debates, these were heart songs to him. He graduated from college and spent three years in "the real world," as he calls it; then he went back to school and received his master's. He admits today he would love to continue on in school indefinitely if he could afford the time. Learning in his early years was for him a way to be able to do things. But now he sees learning as pure enjoyment. "I like an environment where learning is all around me," he says, "a sense of campus where people are all interested in the important issues of life." Community is vitally important to Mario. "And the older I get," he explains, "the more I see my life – if it is to be an important life – must be one of community service."

Format: *the organization,*
plan,
style or
type
of something

—Random House Dictionary

The Evolution of 4MAT

What kind of excellence is possible?

That haunting question has run like a refrain
through my life, my teaching, my research.

Out of that question 4MAT was born
to explore the frontiers of excellence
and, hopefully, to push them even further.
What would happen if the natural learning cycle
were so well understood and used
that people, young and old, could become *authors*
of their own learning process,
creators of their own forms of excellence...

The intuition of 4MAT began as an answer to that question,
as a response to a lifetime quest for equity for every learner.

The name 4MAT comes from the fact
that we have four major learning styles
and that the four quadrants present
different formatting possibilities in turn.

Originally created as
an instructional design model
to address and capitalize
on these four major and very different learning styles,
4MAT's intent is to improve the odds
for as many students as possible.

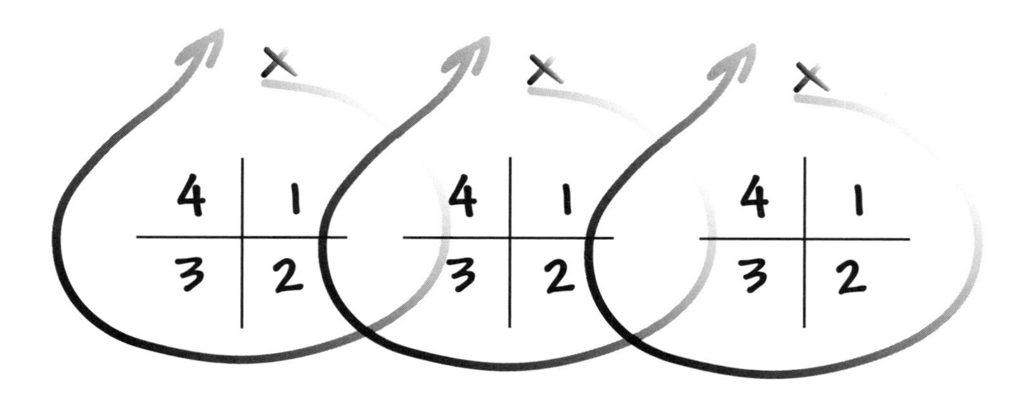
×
4
1
3
2
×
4
1
3
2
×
4
1
3
2

When I created 4MAT,
I worked from known research:
Lewin, Vygotsky, Dewey, Piaget, Bruner, Kolb.
It made sense to me.
It rang true to my long-time classroom experience.
I recognized the diverse learners I had taught.
I had witnessed their struggles as they
compensated for their styles.

I created composite descriptions of the four styles
using Kurt Lewin's experiential learning cycle.

Lewin's overlay of the dimensions
of perceiving and processing
created the four quadrant system.
This system defines four profoundly different parameters
for approaching learning.
I added left- and right-mode processing
to each quadrant,
resulting in a useful instructional design.

My intent was to apply this framework to instruction
in order to appeal to each of the four learning styles in turn,
while alternating teaching strategies
with right- and left-mode techniques.

Cycle: a series of occurrences that repeats
—Random House Dictionary

When I created 4MAT
I believed absolutely
that all learners need to master all of the quadrants.

My experience with 4MAT
over the last fifteen years
has proven that to be true.

Wholeness and balance is the result
if learners learn to function well
in all parts of the cycle.

Many of us recognize this cycle
when we are made aware of it.
We realize that we make personal connections in our lives,
we examine expert knowledge and then define things for ourselves,
we problem-solve, and we refine our problem-solving,
and we adapt and create our own ways of being and doing.

But we need to become ever more aware of it,
so aware that we feel its movement from within.
We need to understand how this cycle works in our lives.

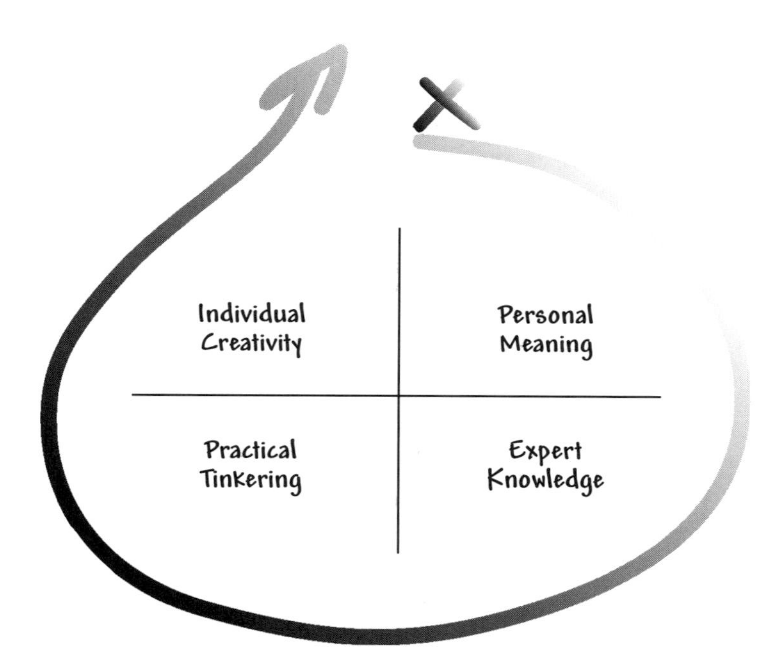
Individual Creativity
Personal Meaning
Practical Tinkering
Expert Knowledge

Learning must be fluid and open
even as it must be structured and closed.
The flow from personal meaning in Quadrant One
back to the integration of the learning in Quadrant Four
allows and encourages individuals
to bring their idiosyncratic adaptations
to the learning act.

The structure inherent
in the expert knowledge in Quadrant Two
and the practice of that knowing
in the heart of Quadrant Three
gives the learner the expertise and confidence
to move into unique, personal adaptations.

Real learning moves
from the personal, perceived connections of Quadrant One,
to the conceptual knowing of Quadrant Two,
to the practice and tinkering of Quadrant Three,
and then to the creative integration of Quadrant Four.

This movement can happen
even as learners move
with the particular gracefulness that comes
from their favorite place on the cycle,
their preferred learning style.

To know: to grasp in the mind
to regard as true beyond doubt
to have a practical understanding of
to have fixed in the mind
to have experience of
to recognize
to be able to distinguish
to discern the character or nature of
to be intimate with

—Random House Dictionary

Knowledge must be used.
It must operate in one's life.

And because all humans are unique,
we use and then integrate learning in our own
inimitable, incomparable ways.

What we learn is transformed into a particular use,
a distinct way of doing,
a matchless refinement of a method,
a unique understanding.

It is transformed.
It becomes for us.

It is in the transformation that real understanding happens.

And it can only happen when we complete the cycle,
when we return to 12 o'clock.

All rising to a great place
is by a winding stair.
— Francis Bacon

I have come to see that it is the cycle
that is the magic,
the cycle that is the major reason for the success of the model.

In the process of going through that cycle,
we learn how to learn.

When the subjectivity of 12 o'clock
is reflected on at 3 o'clock,
ordered and objectified at 6 o'clock,
tried and personalized at 9 o'clock,
and uniquely and creatively integrated into the learner's life
back at 12 o'clock,
then real learning happens.

And the cycle begins anew.

Experience is only half of experience.
— Goethe

4MAT is formed from the rhythm
of the perceiving and processing dimensions
of the natural learning cycle.

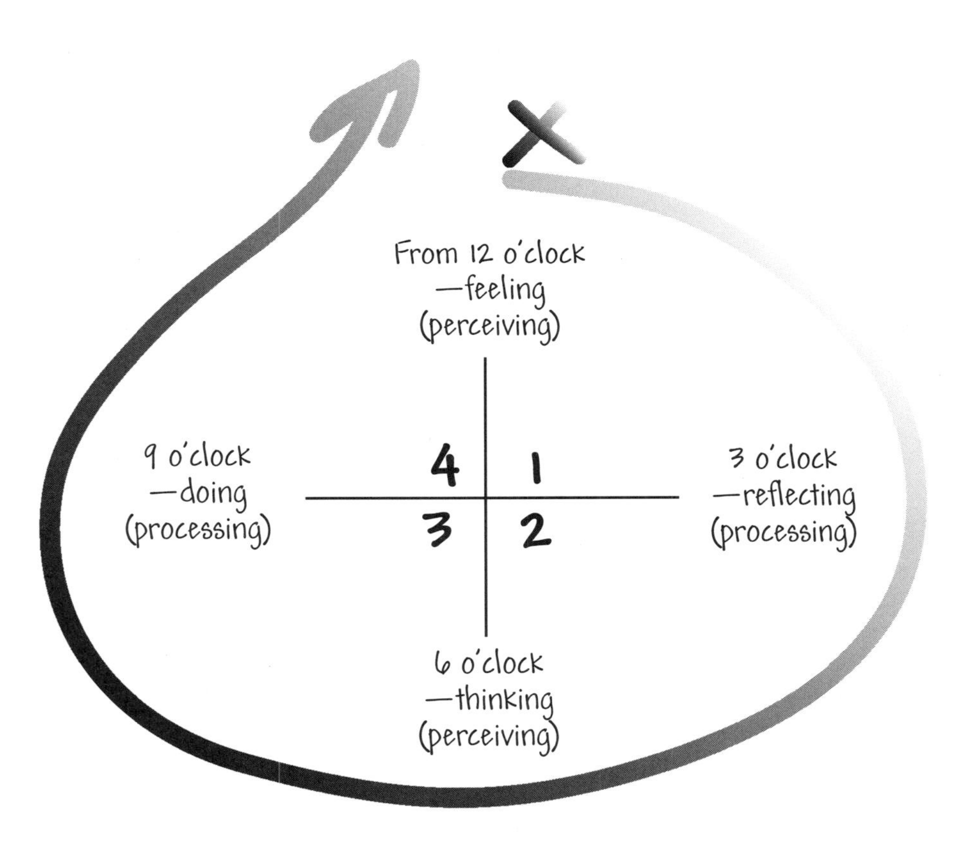

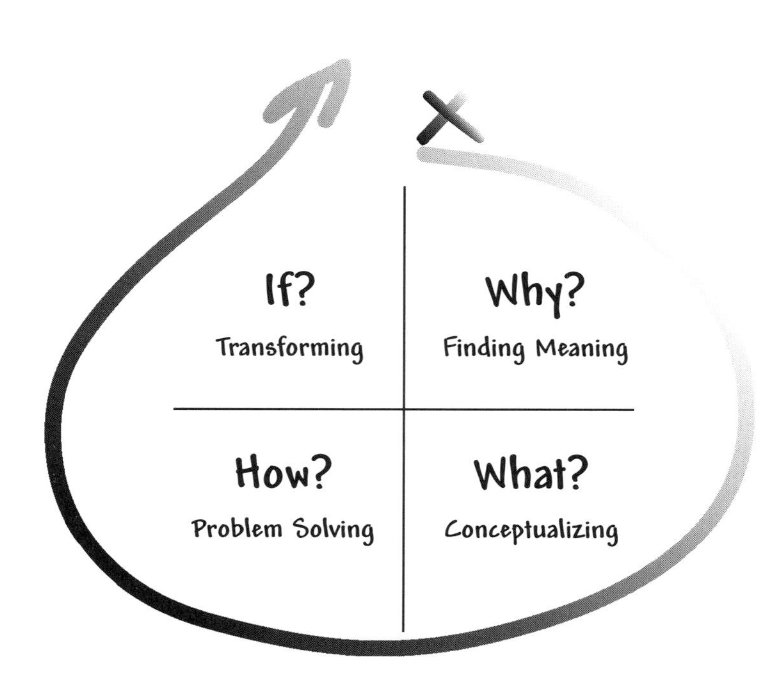
If?
Transforming
Why?
Finding Meaning
How?
Problem Solving
What?
Conceptualizing

These four quadrants embody
the core elements of learning:
feeling, reflecting, thinking and doing.

Oneness combines feeling and reflecting,
the heart of **meaning**.

Twoness combines reflecting and thinking,
the heart of **conceptualization.**

Threeness combines thinking and doing,
the heart of **problem solving**,

and **Fourness** combines doing and feeling,
the heart of **transformation**.

Each of the core elements of learning –
feeling, reflecting, thinking and doing –
elicits a different and crucial question
from the learner.

All successful learning
deals with these four elements
and answers four questions:
Why? What? How? and If?

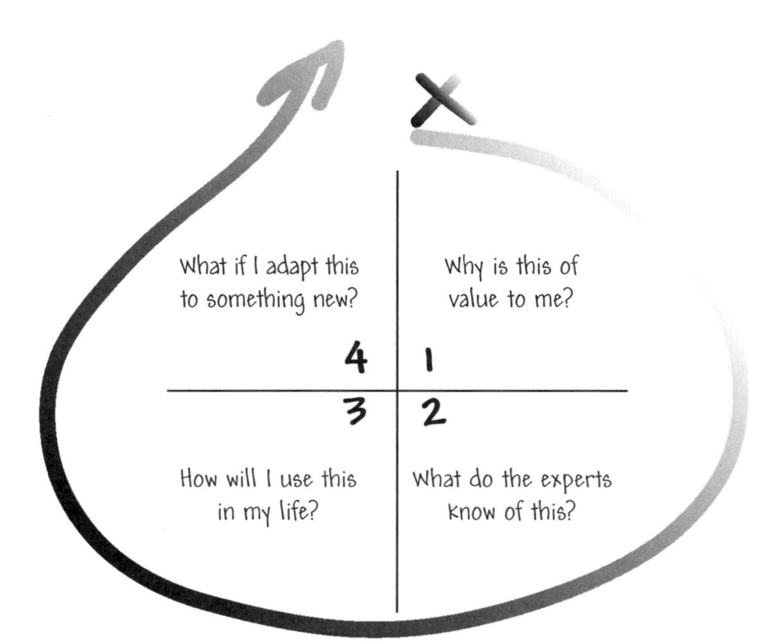
What if I adapt this to something new?
Why is this of value to me?
4
1
3
2
How will I use this in my life?
What do the experts know of this?

In Quadrant One the union of elements creates personal meaning,
the way we question the value of new learning
by connecting it to ourselves.
And the question to be answered is "Why?"
Why is this of value to me?
Why do I sense the need to know this?

In Quadrant Two the union of elements
creates conceptualized content,
structuring knowledge into significant chunks
that form the essence, the coherence, and the wonder of new ideas.
The question to be answered is "What?"
What is out there to be known?
What do the experts know about this?
What is the nature of the knowledge I am pursuing?

In Quadrant Three the union of elements creates usefulness
(and the more immediate the better),
the transferability into one's life,
problem solving with the learning.
The question to be answered is "How?"
How does this work?
Will this streamline my tasks?
How will this be of use in my life?

In Quadrant Four the union of elements creates creative integration,
the way we adapt the learning into something new and unique.
The question to be answered is "What If?"
If I use this in my own way, what will happen?
What can I create and how will that creation
expand, enhance, and maybe even transform the world I know?

In due course we arrive,
if it can be said
that we ever fully arrive.
The truth is there are
destinations beyond destinations,
and so the confirmed sailor
goes on tacking forever.
— Richard Bode

The true love of all dancers
is dancing.
— Gary Zukav

The cycle is the key.
It is the cycle that brings balance
and wholeness to learning.

The cycle forms us from within.
We are all natural-born learners.
Learning is meaning making.
We spend our entire lives in this enterprise.
We attend, we reflect, we understand, we try,
we adapt and we integrate.
And the cycle is the way we learn,
whether we recognize it or not.

We need to answer all four questions,
even though some will always have
more meaning for us than others.

As the learner's style is formed
by moving through the cycle,
different comfort levels occur.
We move from our comfort zones
to the edges of our competence
at different places along the way.
With a supportive environment
we can step more firmly into uncomfortable places,
where wondrous growth awaits.
Clearly, the dance itself is the thing.

Teachers, trainers and learners...
mentors, managers, ministers...
doctors, dancers and docents –
all need to understand this.

Climates and Methods

Each of the four quadrants lends itself to different goals.
The instructional and, interestingly enough, the management methods change as we move through the cycle.

The goal in **Quadrant One** is personal connections – meanings brought from the past into the discussions and conversations, events remembered and connected, fascination experienced, subjectivity honored and explored, insights shared.

The learning climate needs to be easy, open, nurturing:
experiences, storytelling, dialogue,
listening that is interested and focused,
personal space, exploration of meanings,
imagining, inferring, generating ideas.

The method is **Discussion:**
cooperative learning, trust, mutual influence,
high acceptance, sharing, interaction,
experiences understood as personal truths.

The teacher is the initiator, the motivator, capturing enthusiasm.

The learner is receiving.

The goal in **Quadrant Two** is defining the learning –
expert knowledge, the best information,
pertinent facts that are structured and planned,
organizing, patterning, seeing relationships,
prioritizing, classifying and comparing.

The learning climate is receiving, taking in,
being briefed, writing things down,
thoughtfulness, ponderings,
reflections, thinking out loud,
being present to the content.

The method is traditional **"Teaching":**
lectures, demonstrations, films, videos,
speakers, readings, CD-ROM, telecommunicating,
videodiscs, satellite conferencing,
conceptualizing, being skeptical, questions, answers,
and more questions.

The teacher delivers the content,
theorizing, conceptualizing, organizing.

The learner is forming concepts.

Then the focus shifts from the actions of the teacher
to the actions of the students.

The goal in **Quadrant Three** is problem solving –
skills perfected and used,
practicing, experimenting, mastering, predicting,
recording, seeing how things work,
placing learning into one's life.

The learning climate is active, doing,
noting happenings and discrepancies,
trying ideas, seeing from different angles,
finding personal uses for the learning,
tinkering with it.

The method is **Coaching**:
mastery learning, action science,
work stations, laboratory experimenting,
seeing what happens, partnering,
asking questions, checking results,
comparing, reaching conclusions.

The teacher is the coach, in the best sense of that word:
facilitating, nurturing good tries, asking provocative questions,
and setting up environments that encourage experimentation.

The learner is tinkering, testing, trying.

The goal in **Quadrant Four** is refining and creating –
verifying, explaining, summarizing,
adapting, modifying, reworking,
re-presenting, synthesizing,
being fascinated anew.

The learning climate is dynamic, celebratory,
open-ended, renewing, challenging,
boundary-breaking,
modifying and adapting the learning into
something unique.

The method is **Self-Discovery**:
re-presenting, refocusing,
learning independently,
asking better questions,
making new connections.

The teacher is the cheerleader, facilitating independence,
getting resources, championing, promoting.

The learner is acting, adapting, creating.

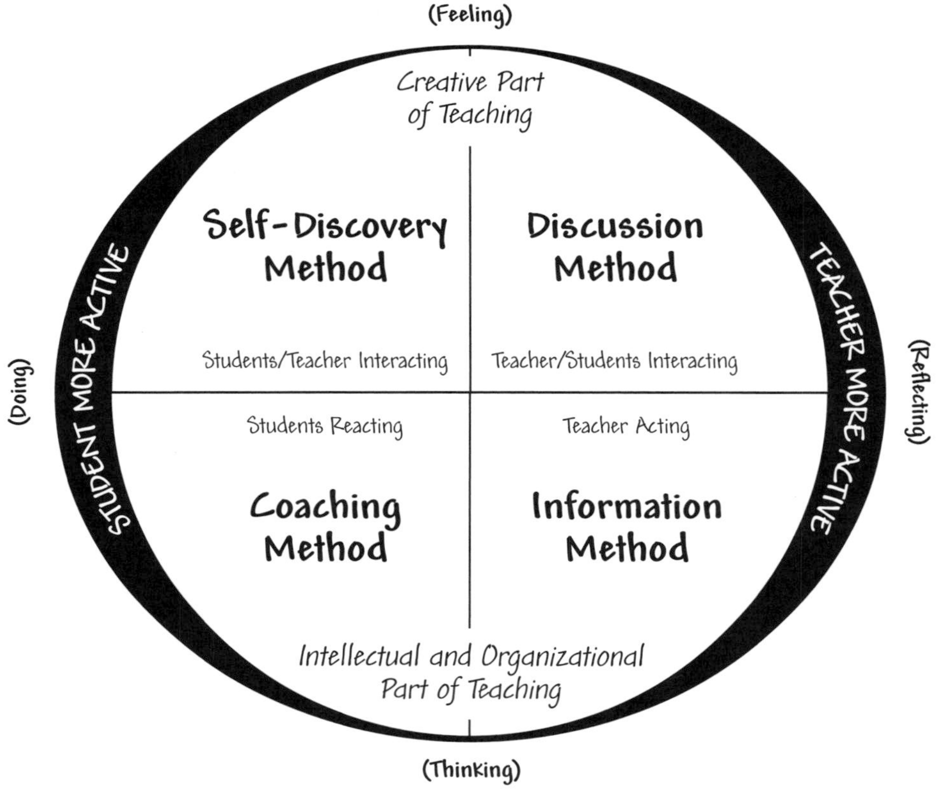

(Feeling)

Creative Part of Teaching

STUDENT MORE ACTIVE

TEACHER MORE ACTIVE

(Doing)

(Reflecting)

Self-Discovery Method

Students/Teacher Interacting

Discussion Method

Teacher/Students Interacting

Students Reacting

Coaching Method

Teacher Acting

Information Method

Intellectual and Organizational Part of Teaching

(Thinking)

In the process of going through that cycle,
from quadrant to quadrant,
we luxuriate in our comfort places
and stretch within those that challenge us.
Even as we do so, we move in harmony
not only with our preferred learning styles
but with our brain hemisphere preferences as well.

An intuitive, synthesizing Right-Mode One Learner
will take a very different approach to a new idea or skill
than a logical, analytic Left-Mode One.

A Type Three Learner putting a bicycle together
with a right-mode approach will not read the instructions
(guaranteed)!
A Left-Mode Three will read the instructions step-by-step
and carefully lay out all the parts.

If we design instruction
to mirror this natural movement,
we move around the cycle,
through the four quadrants
from meaning, to conceptual understanding,
to application, and to adaptation
adding the elements of analysis (left mode)
and the technique of synthesis (right mode) to each quadrant:
synthesizing and analyzing meaning,
synthesizing and analyzing conceptual understanding,
analyzing and synthesizing application,
and analyzing and synthesizing adaptation.
The result is an eight-step model for instructional design
that is a useful framework for learning and teaching,
managing and meeting, preaching and parenting…

This eight-step model forms the 4MAT Cycle.

Don't lose sight of your destination,
for the quest of your life
is to discover who you are.
— Henrik Ibsen

The Eight Words: The Result of the Right/Left Overlay on the Cycle

Quadrant One

Connect: R Mode	Placing ourselves in the presence of the newness by connecting it to our personal experience
Examine: L Mode	Dialoguing experiences analogous to the new learning

Quadrant Two

Image: R Mode	Forming pictures in our minds as we go for the big idea
Define: L Mode	Examining expert knowledge

Quadrant Three

Try: L Mode	Practicing the skills that make the learning useful
Extend: R Mode	Adding our own unique use of it

Quadrant Four

Refine: L Mode	Adapting, modifying, (or sometimes changing what we are learning because it sends us off in a new direction)
Integrate: R Mode	Creating and integrating, completing the cycle while it begins anew

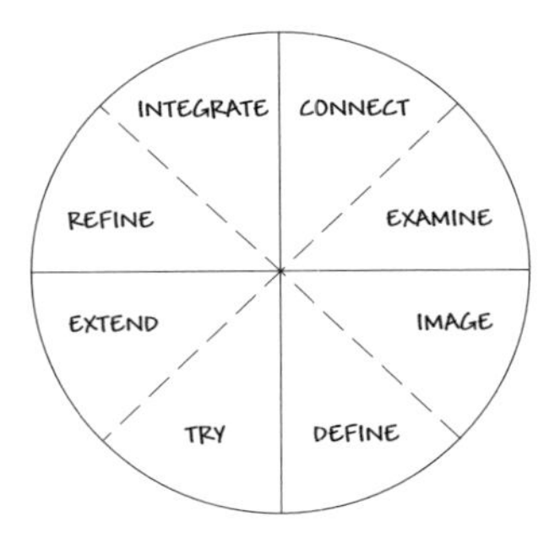

The creativity of my subjects
seemed to be an epiphenomenon
of their greater wholeness and integration,
which is what self-acceptance implies.
— Abraham Maslow

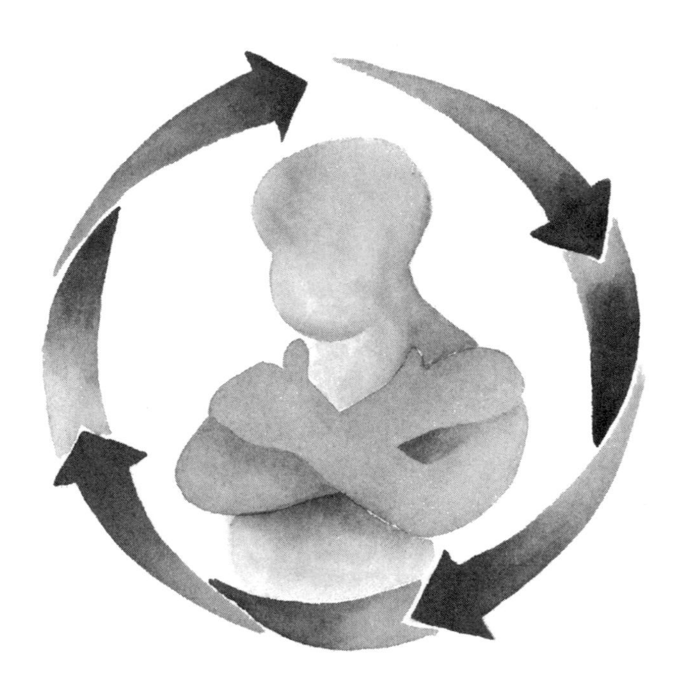

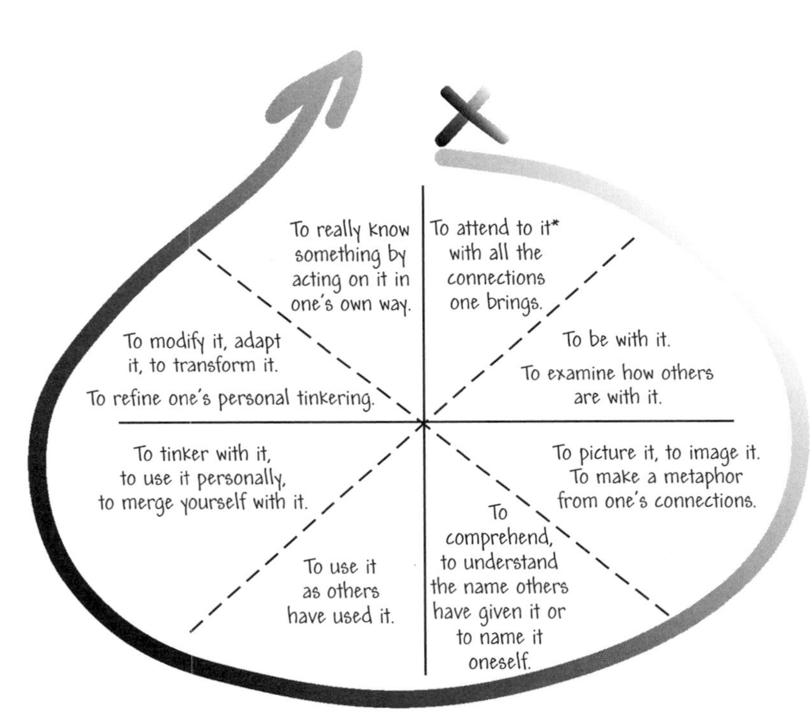

*"It" is any new experience, any new reality coming into the learner's world—a person, an idea, a skill, an event. The possibilities are limitless.

The fox knows many things,
but the hedgehog knows one big thing.

The fox moves on many levels,
seizing upon the essence of experience.
The hedgehog follows a single, organizing principle,
a central vision, one system.

Taken figuratively these words mark
one of the deepest differences
which may divide human beings.
— Isaiah Berlin

The Right-Left Mode Shift in 4MAT

As seen in the various model diagrams,
the rhythm of right- and left-mode strategies
reverses at 6 o'clock.

Just as the teacher's role shifts at 6 o'clock
and the learners become the major actors in the process,
the alternation of right-and left-mode strategies
also shifts at 6 o'clock.

This is the reason why.
The beginning of the cycle starts with experience,
the heart of the right mode,
and moves on to where the teacher
finally stands at 6 o'clock
speaking with the voice of the experts.
This is where she presents the facts,
the issues, the known coherence.

After listening to the expert knowledge
and examining what the experts have described and created,
the learners begin to practice.

They follow in the direct footprints of the experts
as they master the learning
as it is now known and understood.

When they accomplish this,
when they come to understand the learning as it is taught,
mastering the practice
with diligence and thoroughness,
they enter the right-mode world, the world
of personalizing, adapting and recreating.
They begin to blend expert knowing with their own knowing.

Brain lateralization research
has confirmed that there are indeed
two different kinds of cognition.

... we act when an interhemispheric consensus
is reached between our two minds.
— Leonard Shlain

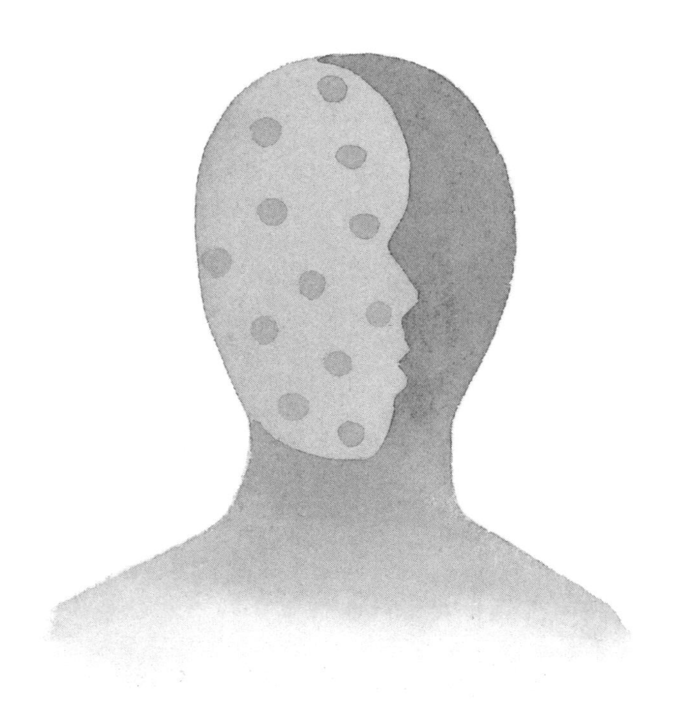

This shift from the expert
and the practice of the expert's way
(left-mode study and application)
to the learner and the learner's way –
(right-mode tinkering and adapting
and doing on the part of the learner)
is absolutely crucial for the movement to 9 o'clock.

9 o'clock is the doing place on the cycle.
It is where learning gets personalized
and transferred into real life.

After the transfer,
the refinement happens.
The left-mode analyzer steps in and edits:
How can I do this better,
use this better,
understand this better,
be this better?

Adaptation moves to creation.
The whole brain is in the act.

And so the rhythm from right to left
and left to right,
from the Self,
to the Experts,
and back to the Self.

Because we are in the world,
we are condemned to meaning.
. . . we witness evey minute
the miracle of related experiences.
And yet nobody knows better than we do
how this miracle is worked,
for we are ourselves this network of relationships.
— Maurice Merleau-Ponty

The leader is more active in Quadrants One and Two,
motivating and witnessing
to the value of the learning,
setting the climate, creating connections
to learners' lives,
delivering the content.

Then at 6 o'clock the shift happens,
a gradual role reversal,
a change in focus.

In Quadrants Three and Four,
learners take over the spotlight.
They become the center of activity:
practicing, experimenting, testing validity.

If this shift does not occur,
(and in many classrooms and work places it does not),
the learning never moves from the leader to the learners.
The leader remains center stage.

Then the learners will say,
"This is what they taught me,"

rather than,
"This is what I discovered."

At the heart of 4MAT lies ongoing discovery.
In the hands of skilled practitioners,
it can be an art form
created by honoring the natural cycle of learning
and eliciting its elements
for conscious manipulation.

Wisdom is meaningless
until our own experience
has given it meaning...
and there is wisdom
in the selection of wisdom.
—Bergen Evans

4MAT clarifies how the criteria for learning change
as an individual moves from place to place:
from meaning connection in Quadrant One,
to concepts in Quadrant Two,
to skills and usefulness in Quadrant Three,
and finally to creative adaptation
and modification in Quadrant Four.

The stretch capability of this model
gives us a context to talk about
individual learning differences
as gifts to be celebrated and strengthened.

To feel and to think in balance,
honoring both,
is to have wisdom.

To reflect and to do in equal measure,
honoring both,
gives our lives the gracefulness of continuous learning.

It is upon the foundation
of honoring differences
that 4MAT, the cycle model,
was built.

We begin life with the world presenting itself
to us as it is.
Someone – our parents, teachers, analysts –
hypnotise us to "see" the world
and construe it in the "right" way.
These others label the world, attach names
and give voices to the beings and events in it,
so that thereafter, we cannot read the world
in any other language
or hear it saying other things to us.

The task is to break the hypnotic spell,
so that we become
undeaf, unblind, and multilingual,
thereby letting the world speak to us in new voices
and write all its possible meanings
in the book of our existence.

Be careful in your choice of hypnotists.
— Sidney Jourard

The true teacher
defends his pupils
against his own personal influence.
— Bronson Alcott

A Word About Models

When a model is useful,
it forms a framework
for thinking about something.

Good models are lenses.
They help us see more clearly.
They raise awareness as to how some things work.

One of the most useful aspects of models
is they create a simple language for
talking about complicated things.

With models we examine the parts,
but we start from the whole.
Coherence simplifies.

There is integrity to a good model.
Its core parts must be stable and generalizable.
But there needs to be lots of room
for users to adapt it to their needs
while still being true to its core meaning.

The ultimate worth of a model
is the way users adapt and modify it
to suit their needs.
As they use it, it becomes more and more theirs,
and so it becomes different.

If it is whole and compelling,
they will say, "We did it ourselves,
our adaptation of it works best for us."

May that be so with 4MAT.

CHAPTER SIX

About Learning in Schools: 4MAT and Education

A Learner's Story

Seng was in high school and he loved it. This surprised him because he had never really liked school before. But this was different. He was in a Fine Arts magnet school and life was good. He had two teachers whose classes were electrifying. Two, imagine! One in a lifetime is the best of luck, and he had two in this one year – jazz with his saxophone and modern dance. His parents were delighted with his newfound enthusiasm for school and so was he. All his grades were going up, not just in jazz and dance. He felt things were connected. He felt good about himself.

The earliest users
of the 4MAT Model
were educators,
women and men who recognized
how they might bring the diversities
of their students to rich harvest.

We began by having teachers discover
their own learning styles.
It was magical.
Audiences immediately recognized
the legitimacy of these differences.

I remember one particular audience,
the American Association of Museums.
I gave a two-hour overview of 4MAT
to eight hundred and eighty
curators, designers, and museum educators.

After they had figured out which style they preferred,
I had the audience move so all the Type One Learners
were up front on my left,
all the Type Two Learners were also up front on my right,
the Threes behind the Ones near the back door
(where they like to be),
and the Fours behind the Twos,
where they milled about talking and visiting.
When I noted that the rest of the audience was
waiting for the Fours to settle down, they did so
with much laughter.

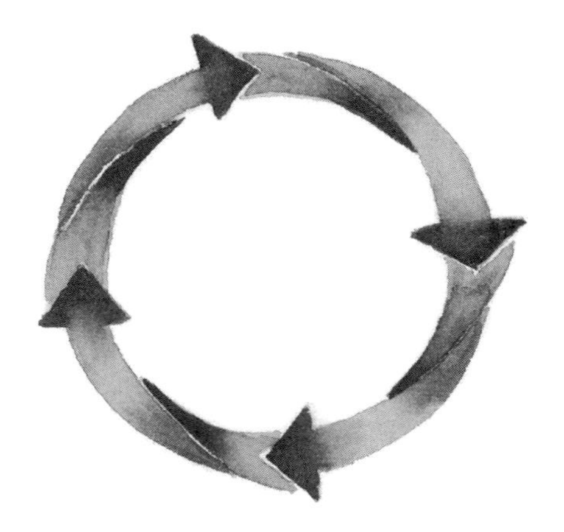

The audience itself proved my point.
As I explained the four learning styles
and the perceiving and processing characteristics of each,
the audience reacted to my words differently
in different sections of the auditorium.
The reactions on the part of some of the audience
puzzled other parts of the audience.

I loved it! They were living their differences
as I explained the research.
The laughter rippled around the room in its own cycle.

This happened over and over again,
as I was met with equal acceptance
in education staff development circles.
Teachers became intrigued by the 4MAT Cycle
after discovering their own styles.
I found that if I began with them, with their styles,
they moved easily into applying what they had discovered
to their students.
They came to see what a difference the design of the cycle
could make for their learners.
This turned out to be the crucial step.
They moved from a focus on their own individual style
to a focus on the cycle.
Which is exactly what we needed.

We and they began together
in early workshops
writing individual lesson plans
and feeling a rush of innovation
and accomplishment
for having gone around the cycle.

Oneness in Schools*

*A loving place, an
affectionate atmosphere,
a safe place is offered.
Individuality of students
is treasured.
Children learn to care
for and cooperate
with one another.
Curriculum is connected
to life experiences.
The making of meaning
is paramount.*

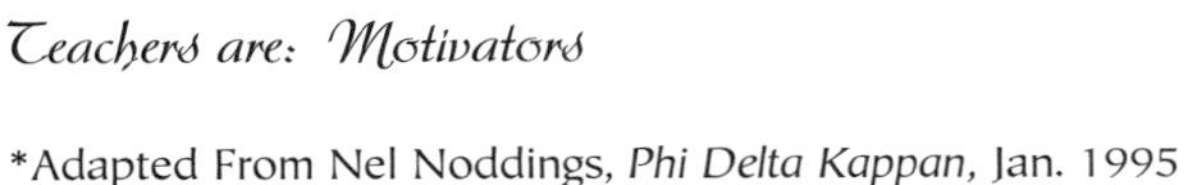

Teachers are: Motivators

*Adapted From Nel Noddings, *Phi Delta Kappan*, Jan. 1995

A Cycle for Instructional Design
A Framework for Successful Teaching

As we began the task of writing 4MAT plans
(a much more difficult task than it looked at first glance),
we discovered that we could extend the conceptualization
of the essence of each Learning Style
to include the climate of the classroom, of the building,
of the district.

We could apply Oneness, Twoness, Threeness, Fourness
to the environment.

The 4MAT Cycle begins with perception,
with the experiences learners bring to the content,
their subjective connections,
their embeddedness (Kegan) in their senses and experiences.

The teacher must create an experience in the classroom
that capitalizes on these perceptions,
these personal connections.

This is accomplished in Quadrant One.

Right- and left-mode strategies
are used in each quadrant.
In Quadrant One, the connecting situation the teacher creates
is first experienced (R mode)
and then the group examines the combined reactions
of the group members (L mode).

Twoness in Schools

Forms of knowing are explored.
Ways of living are explored.
Societal practices are examined.
Literary, artistic achievements are experienced.
Opportunities exist to explore human life questions.
Habits of mind are developed.

Teachers are: Content Experts

Then the content is taught conceptually,
in frameworks that contain the essence.
And if done well, less is more –
important in today's mentality.

Content is the testimony of the experts,
the information students need
so they can fold their subjective experiences
into expert knowing, blending
the two together.

The learners move
from their subjectivity to objectivity,
from being embedded in, subject to their perceptions,
to freeing themselves to differentiate their perceptions,
to have them, to make them objects, not just to be in them.

This is accomplished in Quadrant Two.

We require that the students create a metaphor or an analogy,
some kind of subjective representation of the concept
as they understand it (R mode) before the teacher delivers the lecture,
the knowledge piece (L mode).
This is the student's experience of the concept, their tacit knowing,
before the expert knowing is established.
If the proper connection
has been made in Quadrant One,
students come to the lecture
not as strangers in a strange land,
but rather as those who can say,
"Ah yes, I already understood some of this."

Threeness in Schools

Real activities are going on:
newspapers, interviews,
theater, art exhibitions,
musical performances,
community actions.
Students work together
and alone.
There is respect for
honest work.
Learning is useful.

Teachers are: Coaches

Next the learners get to practice
what they have learned from the expert content.

They connect it back to their own experience,
trying it out and trying it on for themselves,
moving toward a decision about its usefulness to them.

They tinker with it,
they experiment,
they observe what happens in the real world.

This is accomplished in Quadrant Three.

We ask students to practice exactly what they have learned
after the formal presentation of the content (Quadrant Two, L mode).
We ask them to try what they have learned
exactly as the experts know it (Quadrant Three, L mode).
When this is accomplished,
when they have mastered it as it is known,
they are ready for the real proof of learning.
They are ready to do something of their own
with what they have learned (R mode).

Fourness in Schools

Multiple models
for success are offered.
A model of possibilities
for democratic life is practiced.
Self-governing learning
communities grow.
Students develop the
capacity to sustain
uncertainty, to take risks.
High belief in wonder
and awe exists.
Entrepreneurial spirit is fostered.
Multiple methods of assessment
are used.

Teachers are: Co-evaluators

Finally, the learners make use of the learning.
They do this by examining its place in their lives,
its transferability.

They are given a range of experiences
to work from –
options for representing their use of the learning,
options with enough diversity
to ensure that each learner's voice
can speak with strength and originality.

The new learning is refined and adapted
into something unique for them,
something they will use in their own way.
They integrate it.

"An old center that once was them is lost,
and a new center is found." (Kegan)

Boredom, the worst obstacle to learning,
cannot happen here –
not if the learner can feel herself en route
to a place where there are always clearings,
possibilities of new openings.

This is accomplished in Quadrant Four.

They refine and edit their findings (L mode)
and then adapt and integrate the learning into their lives (R mode).
Then the cycle can begin again, renewing the learning
at higher and higher levels.

Meaning-making is a history of transformations.
— Robert Kegan

When right- and left-mode approaches to learning –
whole to part and part to whole,
synthesis and analysis,
round and linear,
metaphoric and literal –
are added to each of the four quadrants,
they bring further balance and wholeness
to the instructional design.

The emphasis schools place on left-mode thinking –
on embracing analysis,
looking at parts,
delineating cause-and-effect relationships,
gathering facts, examining pros and cons –
neglects the right mode, and its nonverbal forms
of receiving, integrating, and representing knowledge as well as its

tendencies to:
find and create spatial relationships,
perceive wholes from collections of parts,
learn by doing with hands-on tasks,
take insight and intuition seriously,
form mind pictures to understand the big idea.

The function of poetry is
to say in words
what words cannot say.
— Elliot Eisner

If I read a book
and it makes my body so cold
no fire can ever warm me,
I know that is poetry.

If I feel physically
as if the top of my head
were taken off,
I know that is poetry.

These are the only ways I know it.
Is there any other way?
— Author Unknown

The difference between
the right word and the almost right word
is the difference between
lightning and lightning bug.
— Mark Twain

Because the big picture is often nameless
and our intuitive hunches are sometimes clamorous,
we recognize that many of our knowings are tacit, inexpressible.
We see ourselves making decisions based on tones of meetings,
on the context of events, on unspoken meanings.

When we attempt to describe what these knowings are,
we are often frustrated.
And we are aware of the love affair our culture has
with the precise word,
a culture that grants wallflower treatment to right-mode expression,
even many times ignoring the work of the poets, musicians and visual
artists among us.

Distinct things we can specify, point out, delineate
are one thing, common to us all,
but to hold something in your mind
unable to put it into words,
even while it permeates the moment,
is the most human of happenings as well.

It is the balance of both modes –
so essential for excellence –
that educators must seek.
Meaning is multiple,
and so should be the forms by which we seek it
and represent it.

Classroom applications of 4MAT
are included in Appendix A, page 405.

Some Thoughts on Assessment: A Conversation That Must Take Place Around the Wheel

Even a cursory view of the evaluation aspects
of the lesson plan wheels in Appendix A
makes it clear that traditional assessment
will not suffice for teaching around the cycle.
How do we assess learner progress around the wheel?
Traditional methods work fairly well for
Quadrants Two and Three
but not at all well in Quadrants One and Four.

The writers of the units presented
measured how well their learners knew the facts.
They also assessed how well their students understood the concepts,
how well they could manage the practice requirements,
how well their skills were progressing.

But they added some new and equally important assessments,
the connections students were making
based on their own experiences,
the learning transfers they were making into their own real lives
(not just their instructional lives),
the adaptations they were making and the creations they were forging,
how they were blending expert knowledge with their own.

Our chief task as educators
is to help learners
come to use and adapt what they learn,
to bring them back to themselves,
so they begin to speak
more and more confidently in their own voices.

How much do students really love to learn,
to persist, to passionately attack
a problem or a task?
... to watch some of their prized ideas
explode and to start anew?
... to go beyond being merely dutiful
or long-winded?

Let us assess such things.
— Grant Wiggins

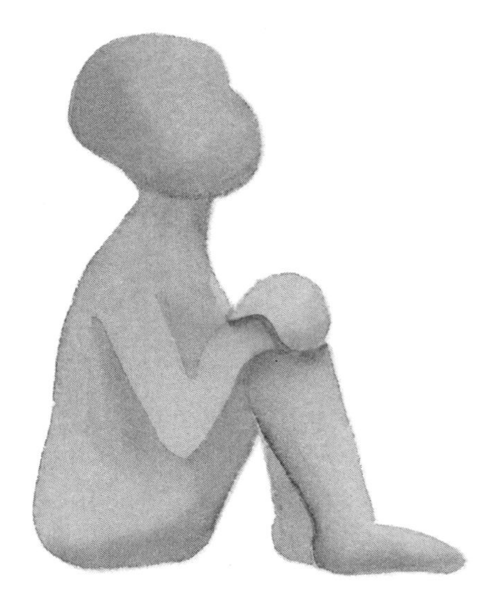

Voices are groomed and encouraged
foremost in dialogue,
by serious listening and learning,
by internalizing our experiences,
attending to the experts in our lives,
being attuned to our culture,
listening to our hearts and
examining with our minds.

We remember the day when we startled ourselves
with the sound of our own voice,
the day when we first spoke out.

How do we come one day to speak in our own voice,
to dare a conversation with the world?
Where do we get the courage to be in dialogue?

We get this courage from thoughtful listeners,
authentic interactors,
people who encourage us and fiercely guard our right
to come one day to speak in our own voice.

Speak what you think now
in hard words,
and tomorrow, speak what tomorrow thinks
in hard words again,
though it contradict
everything you said today.
— Ralph Waldo Emerson

I believe this conversation is the heart of assessment.

Assessment is the conversation that takes place
first, within me as I receive the world,
then with others as we share our worlds,
then between my teacher and me,
as I learn the world of the experts,
and finally between me and my work.

This final conversation
ultimately becomes the one
I have on a continuing basis with the world.

If judgments of my work are always external,
I will be dependent on the judges, not myself.
The judgment needs to be internalized.
I need to establish the authority of my own voice,
to make judgments about my own work.

Teachers must create openings that allow them
to enter into their students' work.
They must get to their students' reflections.
To do so they must develop their own reflective habits of mind.
They must explore the subtle nuances of students' development.
This is more complicated than grading,
it takes a much broader range of skills.

— Bena Kallick

Piaget's principal belief was
that this ongoing conversation
between the becoming human being and the world
was central to the nature of all living things.

Kegan believes this conversation is
the very source of thought and feeling,
the development of knowing,
the balance between subject and object.
An eternal conversation.

I am saying this conversation,
the one Piaget and Kegan speak of,
is the assessment act.

Assessment literally means
to sit beside as an assistant judge—

to engage in an authentic dialogue
about the learning that is taking place.

The key piece in this is, of course,
that in order to engage in conversation
the learner, the one being *assisted to judgment*
much more than being judged,
must have a voice,
a deeply personal voice.

Conversation is the laboratory and workshop of the student.

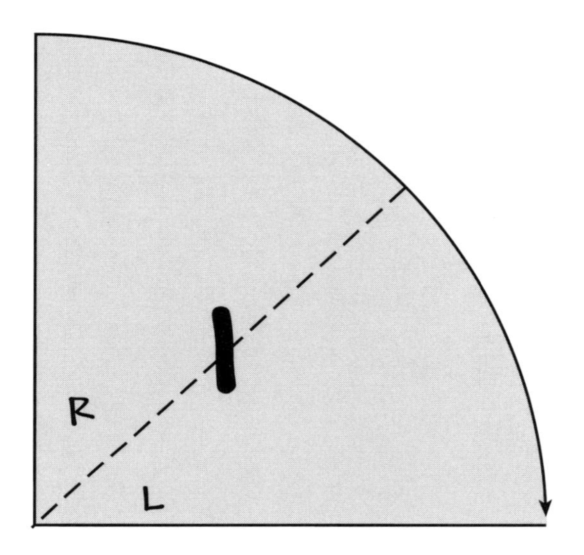

My Voice in Dialogue with Myself and Others
Quadrant One, Right Mode and Left Mode

Listening
Assimilating and reflecting my experiences
and the experience of others
Expressing of feelings and thoughts
Contributing to the group

The 4MAT Cycle moves from my receiving the world,
my listening and feeling the world,
to dialoguing with myself and others about the world,
and finally to my own voice.

Steps One and Two in Quadrant One,
Right Mode and Left Mode,
if properly designed,
will create this kind of dialogue.

I find out what I feel and think
about my experiences
when others are willing to dialogue with me
about what they feel and think
and listen to me about what I feel and think.

It is this dialogue that leads me out
of my embeddedness in my own perceptions
and guides me to see how I have been
held captive by them.
It is this dialogue that helps me to internalize
what I have felt and experienced.

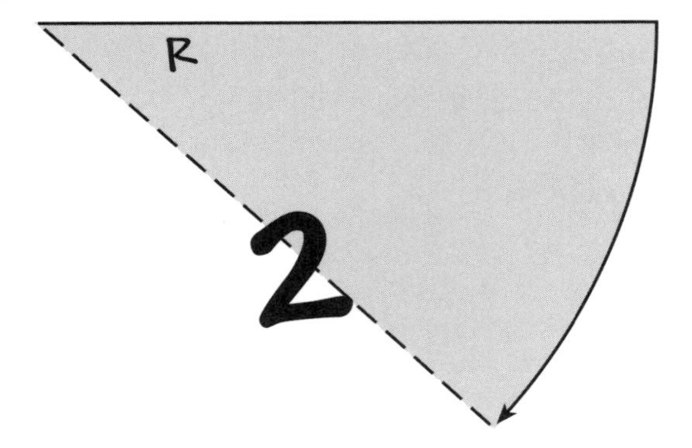

An Image or a Metaphor for the Concept
Quadrant Two, Right Mode

Conceptualizing with originality and congruence
Creating images and metaphors for the concept

When in Quadrant Two, Right Mode of the 4MAT Cycle
I create the image or the metaphor for the concept,
I create a connection.

My subjective understanding of the concept,
encapsulated in the image or the metaphor,
becomes itself an internalized conceptualization that
leads me out of myself and into a more objective place
where I can separate myself from my own views
and examine them along with those of the experts.

In order to do this,
to create a metaphor, an image,
I must move from my feelings and experiences
to examining those feelings and experiences.
I must move from subject to object.

Quadrant Two, Right Mode,
begins the change of focus,
the act of moving out of myself toward objectivity,
to a world other than me,
a world perhaps quite different from my experience.
The metaphor of my experience that I create
enables me to step away from it, better to see it.
It is a separation movement.

Then I attend to the voices of the experts.
My own voice is now silent.
It is time to sit and listen.

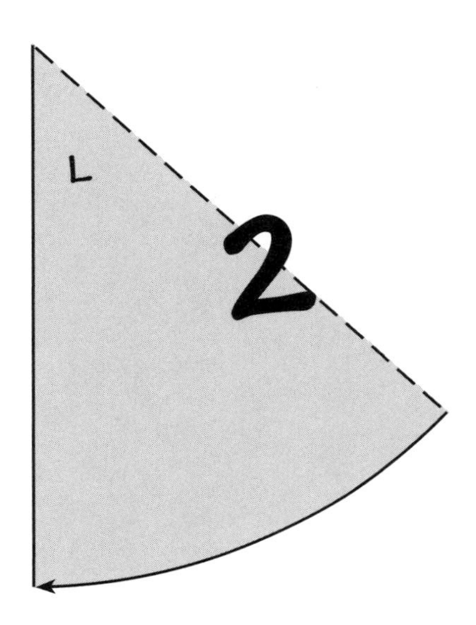

"Listening" to the Voices of the Experts
Assessment: Quadrant Two, Left Mode

Understanding conceptually
Seeing the big picture, the connections,
the interrelationships
Mastering important factual data

In Quadrant Two, Left Mode,
I sit and listen.
I take in the experts, I hear them,
I study them, I attend to them.
I try to see through their eyes,
I examine the process by which they arrived
at what they seem to know.
Many times I am awed by what I hear and see,
sometimes upset by it.
And, if I am lucky, what I hear and see connects
back to my own life.

I confirm my conceptualization,
the connection to my experience,
the image from my particular,
already-present knowledge of the content.
If I am lucky,
I then come to the expert view of the content
more comfortable than I realized,
as someone who can say,
"I think I already knew that.
Yes, I knew that in some small, other way."

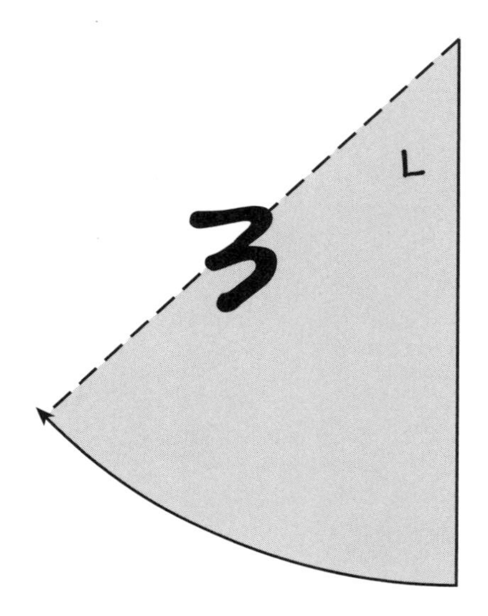

"Practicing" the Experts' Way
Assessment: Quadrant Three, Left Mode

Learning accuracy
Acquiring skills

In Quadrant Three, Left Mode,
I begin to practice as the experts practiced.
I do as they did, slowly, a little at a time,
until I have mastered enough
to put my own spin on things.
And slowly, if I stay with it,
that is exactly what happens.

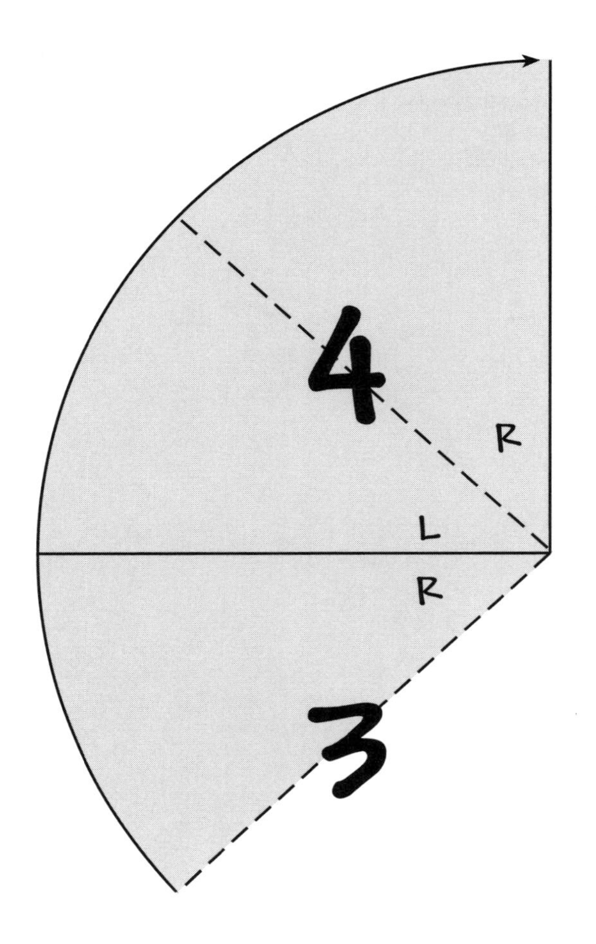

In My Own Voice

Assessment: Quadrant Three, Right Mode
Quadrant Four, Left and Right Modes

Using higher-order thinking skills
Problem-solving
Overviewing
Showing originality and flair
Asking better questions
Having an impact on listeners/readers

If I stay with the emerging conversation,
my own voice deepens and grows richer.
It is then that I begin to use what I have learned,
to blend it, to mold it, to adapt it,
to integrate it.
This place, this eight o'clock place in the cycle,
is where I begin to create something of my own
from what I have learned.

From eight o'clock to twelve o'clock
I must prove my knowing.
I must blend the connections, the content,
and now the use of this new learning
into something that is of me.

The assessment of my work,
how I will be judged,
will now be based on how I **perform**,
on what I can do with what I have learned,
what I have to say now in my own voice.

And it needs to be excellent,
of high quality,
and worth doing.

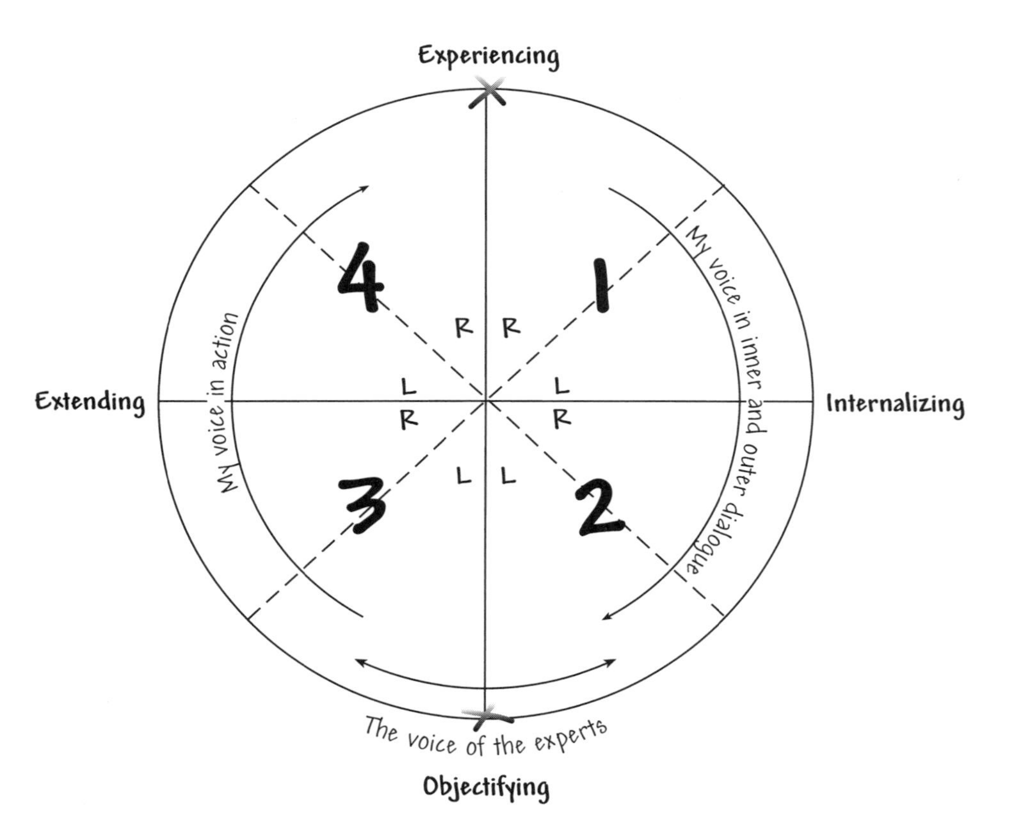
Experiencing
Internalizing
Objectifying
Extending
1
2
3
4
R
R
L
R
L
R
L
L
My voice in inner and outer dialogue
The voice of the experts
My voice in action

The teacher's challenge in all of this,
to truly assess what has been learned
and accomplished,
is to develop a picture of the whole person
while guiding and pointing the way to excellence.

Teachers must use multiple dimensions,
multiple sources,
multiple decision makers,
make multiple observations,
offer multiple options
to develop multiple literacies,

remembering that my voice is multiple as well:
I can speak with words,
with signs,
with symbols,
with movement,
with music.

The more voices I master,
the more representations I create,
the more my learning will be understood
and of value to others,
the more new learning will be created.

Our thinking is shaped
by the media we use to re-present it.
We need to be multiple thinkers.

Here
it is Alleluiah
en route.
There
it is Alleluiah
on arriving home.
—St. Augustine

At the Gate	On the Way

To measure what was done	To perfect a process
Measurement	Description
Quantitative	Qualitative
Did we do what we tried to do?	Ongoing reaction to treatment with an eye to developing it
Data for reporting – leading to goal-setting for next time	Data for growth – goal-setting while doing it
What did you learn?	Where are you in the learning of this?
Completion	Developmental
A snapshot	A video
"ed"	"ing"

Two Important and Very Different Kinds of Assessments

There are two different kinds of assessments,
two different conversations.

One is to see how the learner is doing;
the other is to find out what has been learned.
One is "On the Way."
The other is "At the Gate."

Teachers and trainers need to understand
the difference between these two methods
of assessment
and use them in balance.

"On the Way" refers to how I am developing,
how I am coming along in my learning of this.

If you are my trumpet teacher,
you are helping me to perfect my fingering,
my mouthpiece work,
my tonal quality.
You are guiding me "On my Way."
Hopefully, there are a lot of "good work!" comments.
There is a lot of encouragement for good tries,
for good practice.

But when I am asked to play the trumpet
in order to move up to first chair
where the most skilled trumpet player would sit,
then I'm on my own.
I must perform or not move up to first chair.
My teacher can only watch.
This assessment is an "At the Gate" assessment.

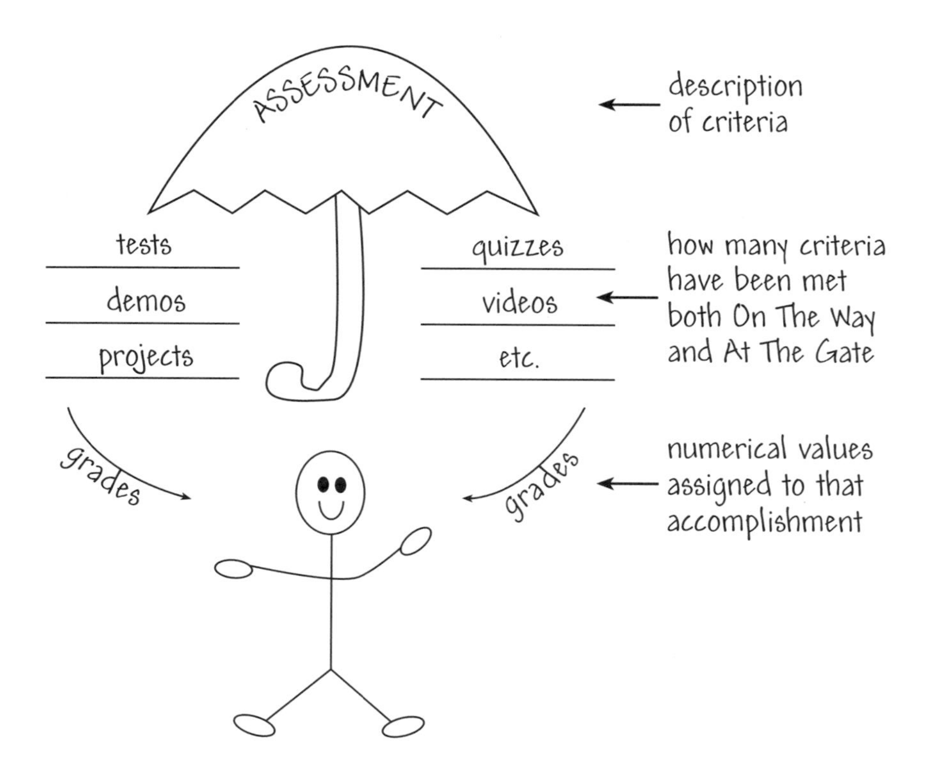
ASSESSMENT
tests
demos
projects
quizzes
videos
etc.
grades
grades
description of criteria
how many criteria have been met both On The Way and At The Gate
numerical values assigned to that accomplishment

If you are teaching me math
and I get a 62 out of a possible 100 on the first quiz
because I have not mastered the process yet,
and then get a 73 on the second quiz
because I have moved further along,
but still don't really get it...but then my practice pays off,
and I get 96 on the exam, please do not average those three grades.
Two were On the Way, and one was At the Gate.
They measure different things; they cannot be averaged together.

Teachers must understand the differences between

assessment, the umbrella that describes and compares to criteria,

and **testing** that determines how many of those criteria have been met,

and **grades** that assign a numerical value to that accomplishment.

**The attitude of teachers must be
to develop the conversations that
lead students ultimately back to themselves.**

Beware of too many At the Gates
and not enough On the Ways.
Elementary schools have far too many At the Gates.

It is the balance of the two
that we must seek.

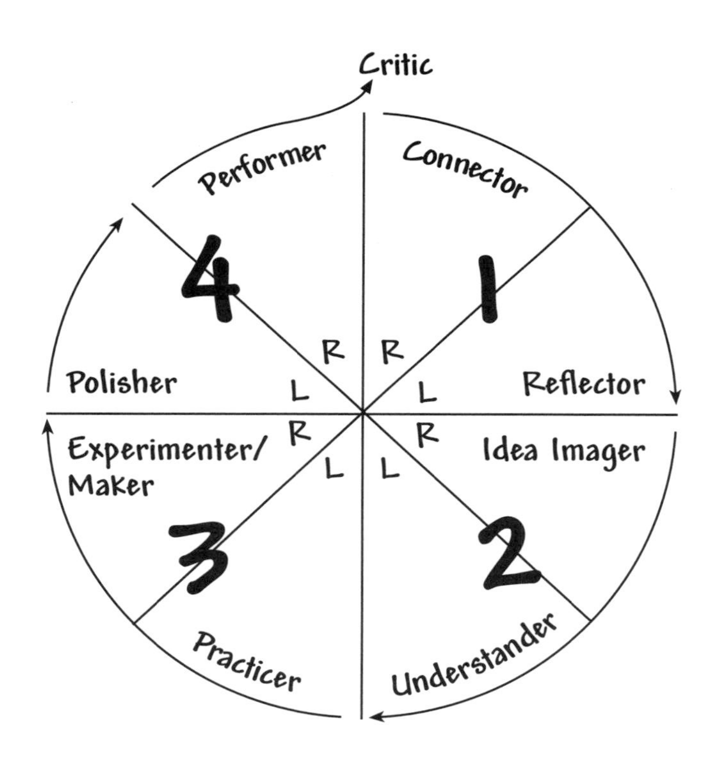
Critic
Performer
Connector
4
1
R
R
Polisher
L
L
Reflector
R
R
Experimenter/
Maker
Idea Imager
L
L
3
2
Practicer
Understander

To assess in a wholistic manner,
teachers must also understand
that the student changes roles
as she moves around the wheel.
Different places on the wheel
require different skills and activities.

These changes are changes in performance
and they are developmental.
The student moves closer and closer
to the ability to integrate the learning,
from connecting,
to reflecting on the connections,
to imaging the concept based on her unique experiences,
to understanding what the experts mean,
to practicing the concepts,
to experimenting, then making something of the learning,
to polishing what she has made/done,
to performing the learning,
and finally to critiquing her results.

Different skills, different learnings, different assessments.

The following two pages illustrate the construct,
goals, student activities, and teacher assessment criteria
for each of the four quadrants.

Although certain goals favor certain quadrants,
they are fluid
and flow through every quadrant.

The goals include attitudes, knowledge,
skills and extensions.

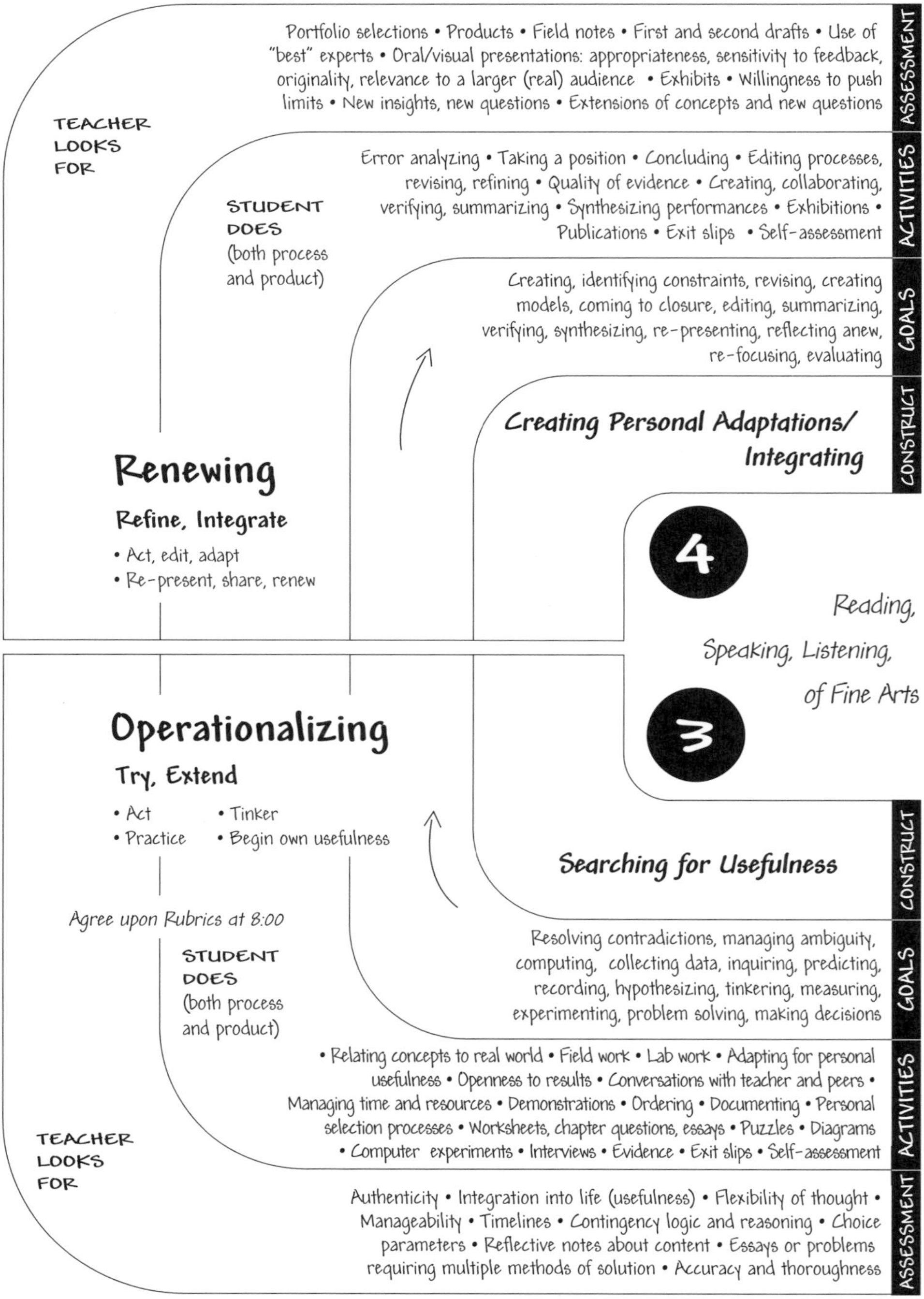

ASSESSMENT

TEACHER LOOKS FOR

Portfolio selections • Products • Field notes • First and second drafts • Use of "best" experts • Oral/visual presentations: appropriateness, sensitivity to feedback, originality, relevance to a larger (real) audience • Exhibits • Willingness to push limits • New insights, new questions • Extensions of concepts and new questions

ACTIVITIES

STUDENT DOES (both process and product)

Error analyzing • Taking a position • Concluding • Editing processes, revising, refining • Quality of evidence • Creating, collaborating, verifying, summarizing • Synthesizing performances • Exhibitions • Publications • Exit slips • Self-assessment

GOALS

Creating, identifying constraints, revising, creating models, coming to closure, editing, summarizing, verifying, synthesizing, re-presenting, reflecting anew, re-focusing, evaluating

CONSTRUCT

Creating Personal Adaptations/ Integrating

Renewing

Refine, Integrate

- Act, edit, adapt
- Re-present, share, renew

4

Reading, Speaking, Listening, of Fine Arts

3

Operationalizing

Try, Extend

- Act
- Practice
- Tinker
- Begin own usefulness

CONSTRUCT

Searching for Usefulness

Agree upon Rubrics at 8:00

GOALS

Resolving contradictions, managing ambiguity, computing, collecting data, inquiring, predicting, recording, hypothesizing, tinkering, measuring, experimenting, problem solving, making decisions

ACTIVITIES

STUDENT DOES (both process and product)

• Relating concepts to real world • Field work • Lab work • Adapting for personal usefulness • Openness to results • Conversations with teacher and peers • Managing time and resources • Demonstrations • Ordering • Documenting • Personal selection processes • Worksheets, chapter questions, essays • Puzzles • Diagrams • Computer experiments • Interviews • Evidence • Exit slips • Self-assessment

ASSESSMENT

TEACHER LOOKS FOR

Authenticity • Integration into life (usefulness) • Flexibility of thought • Manageability • Timelines • Contingency logic and reasoning • Choice parameters • Reflective notes about content • Essays or problems requiring multiple methods of solution • Accuracy and thoroughness

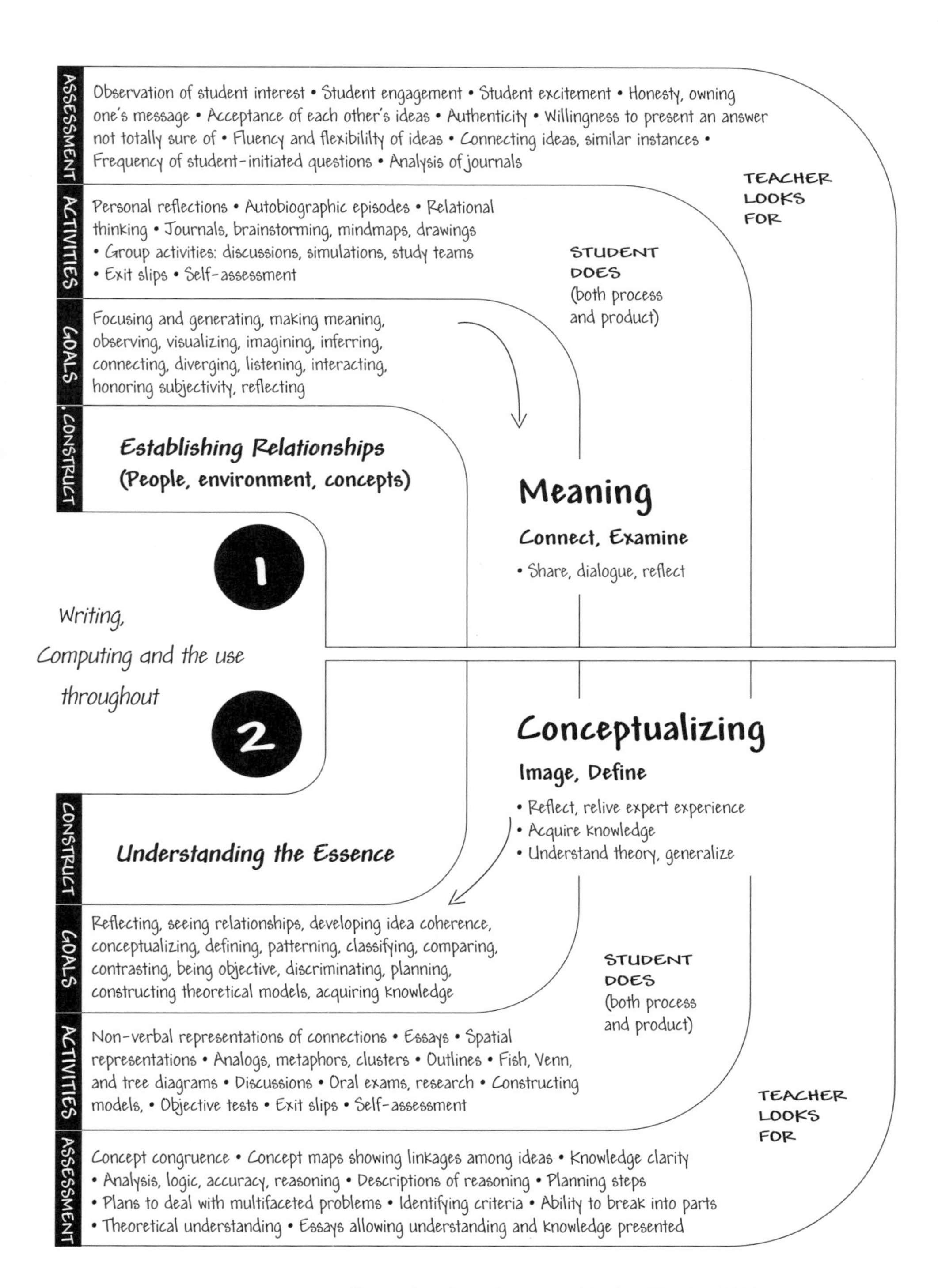
ASSESSMENT
Observation of student interest • Student engagement • Student excitement • Honesty, owning one's message • Acceptance of each other's ideas • Authenticity • Willingness to present an answer not totally sure of • Fluency and flexibililty of ideas • Connecting ideas, similar instances • Frequency of student-initiated questions • Analysis of journals
TEACHER LOOKS FOR
ACTIVITIES
Personal reflections • Autobiographic episodes • Relational thinking • Journals, brainstorming, mindmaps, drawings • Group activities: discussions, simulations, study teams • Exit slips • Self-assessment
STUDENT DOES (both process and product)
GOALS
Focusing and generating, making meaning, observing, visualizing, imagining, inferring, connecting, diverging, listening, interacting, honoring subjectivity, reflecting
CONSTRUCT
Establishing Relationships (People, environment, concepts)
Meaning
Connect, Examine
• Share, dialogue, reflect
1
Writing, Computing and the use throughout
2
Conceptualizing
Image, Define
• Reflect, relive expert experience
• Acquire knowledge
• Understand theory, generalize
CONSTRUCT
Understanding the Essence
GOALS
Reflecting, seeing relationships, developing idea coherence, conceptualizing, defining, patterning, classifying, comparing, contrasting, being objective, discriminating, planning, constructing theoretical models, acquiring knowledge
STUDENT DOES (both process and product)
ACTIVITIES
Non-verbal representations of connections • Essays • Spatial representations • Analogs, metaphors, clusters • Outlines • Fish, Venn, and tree diagrams • Discussions • Oral exams, research • Constructing models, • Objective tests • Exit slips • Self-assessment
TEACHER LOOKS FOR
ASSESSMENT
Concept congruence • Concept maps showing linkages among ideas • Knowledge clarity • Analysis, logic, accuracy, reasoning • Descriptions of reasoning • Planning steps • Plans to deal with multifaceted problems • Identifying criteria • Ability to break into parts • Theoretical understanding • Essays allowing understanding and knowledge presented

It is important
that students bring
a certain ragamuffin barefoot irreverence
to their studies;
they are not here to worship what is known,
but to question it.
— Jacob Bronowski, *The Ascent of Man*

The cycle is old.
It is evident everywhere.

Humans have been learning this way for a long time.

We always begin with meaning
and the end is to come back to ourselves,
to speak in our own voice.

Along the way,
we experience our world,
we dialogue with ourselves and others,
we form pictures in our minds,
we attend to the experts,
we practice,
we personalize,
we integrate,
then we remember.

It is natural to learn this way.

In the process of my coming to understand
the natural learning cycle,
I kept feeling I had always known it.
I found myself recognizing how I had used it
intuitively in much of my teaching.

For the work of the researchers
who helped me bring this cycle to my consciousness,
I am grateful because now I can name it,
now I can own it.

CHAPTER SEVEN

About Learning at Work: 4MAT and the Learning Organization

A Learner's Story

When Nikkie was in junior high school, she played a fine game of basketball. Her coach was her heroine and she loved her time on the court. As far as her other school work went, she enjoyed math and science most, because those two teachers believed problem-solving was the best way to learn. She realized that, in order to enjoy learning, she needed teachers who allowed her to participate, rather than the ones who stood and lectured. Writing was her least favorite task until she had a teacher in college who taught creative writing, a subject she would have avoided at all costs if it had not been required. This teacher took the time to walk her through the process, to guide her step-by-step into the act of writing, from mind-mapping to the finished product. She reports as an adult that she remembers with great fondness those teachers who were process-oriented and whose classes were participatory; she actually remembers most of them by name. She graduated from college with a degree in engineering and even today relishes laboratory situations where real problems are solved under time pressures. She still avoids, at almost all costs, seminars where lecture and passive receiving is the dominant mode of learning.

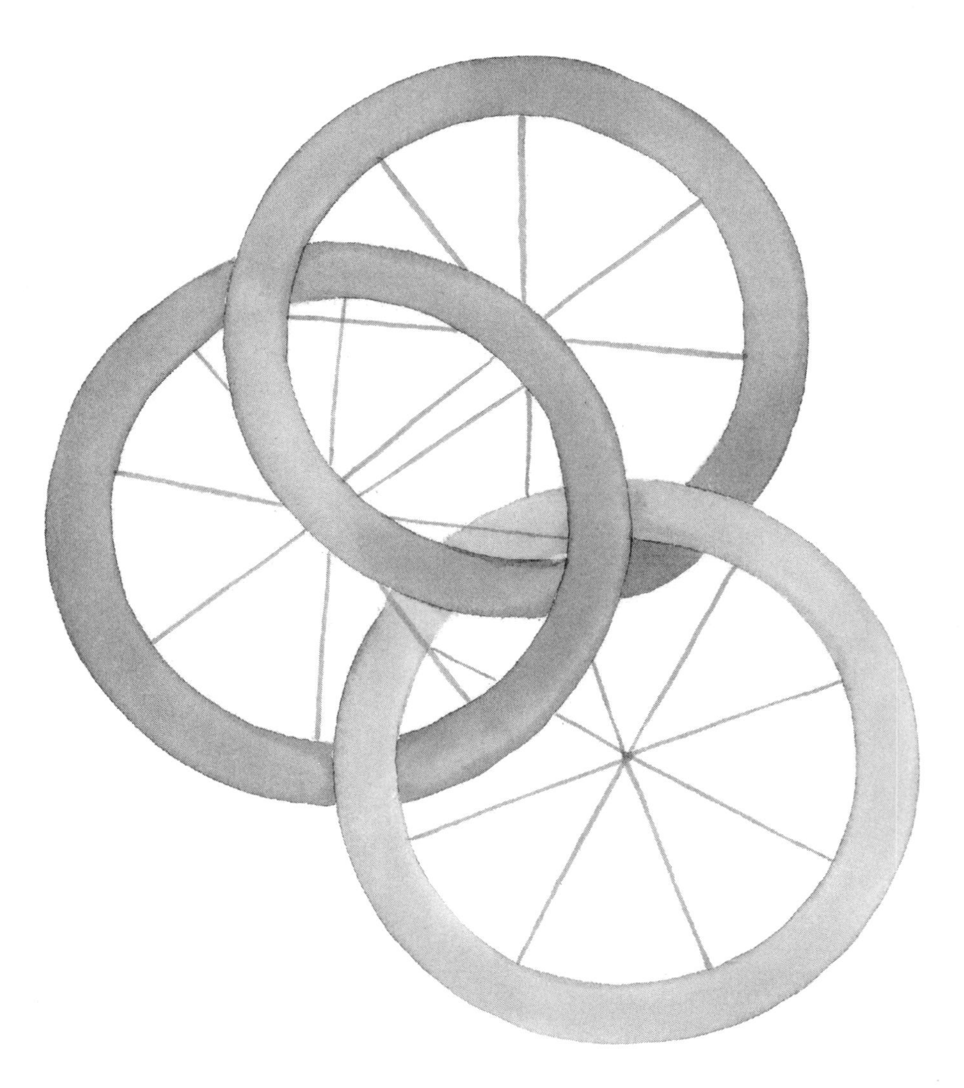

The earliest users of the 4MAT Model
perceived what a difference
cycle knowing
could make for learners everywhere.
We discovered growing balance and wholeness
in the hearts and lives of our learners
as well as in our own.
We sensed ancient origins
within the rhythmic, patterned simplicity
of the wheel and interlocking wheels.

In our audiences and in our work
some interesting questions began to surface:

If this cycle knowing
could make such a real difference
in a child's life, why not in our own?
Honoring diversity and balance,
stretching from comfort to challenge,
does not end with a formal education.

The more freedom in self-organization,
the more order.
— Erich Jantsch

What personal and professional benefits
could be gained for people
if we began to use the 4MAT learning model
in other arenas?

Could learning how to learn
bring discipline, balance
and perhaps transformation to an organization?

The challenge for us
is to see beyond the innumerable fragments
to the whole,
stepping back far enough to appreciate
how things move and change as a coherent entity.
— Margaret Wheatley

If 4MAT were applied successfully to
problem solving and decision making,
would it bring the same balance we had seen in teaching?

Could team building be more effective
if members had different kinds of strengths –
some in communicating and processing,
others in planning and organizing,
others in focusing on the bottom line,
and still others in creative risk taking?

Could communication be enhanced
if people understood and valued these differences?

Could 4MAT be a tool for the development
of leadership skill
with its twin tasks of managing and mentoring?

Are outstanding leaders those who
combine the gifts and skills of all four quadrants?

As the universal nature of the cycle
became increasingly apparent to me,
so did its multiple applications.

Learning does not occur unless
you continuously go back to reality.
— Ray Strata

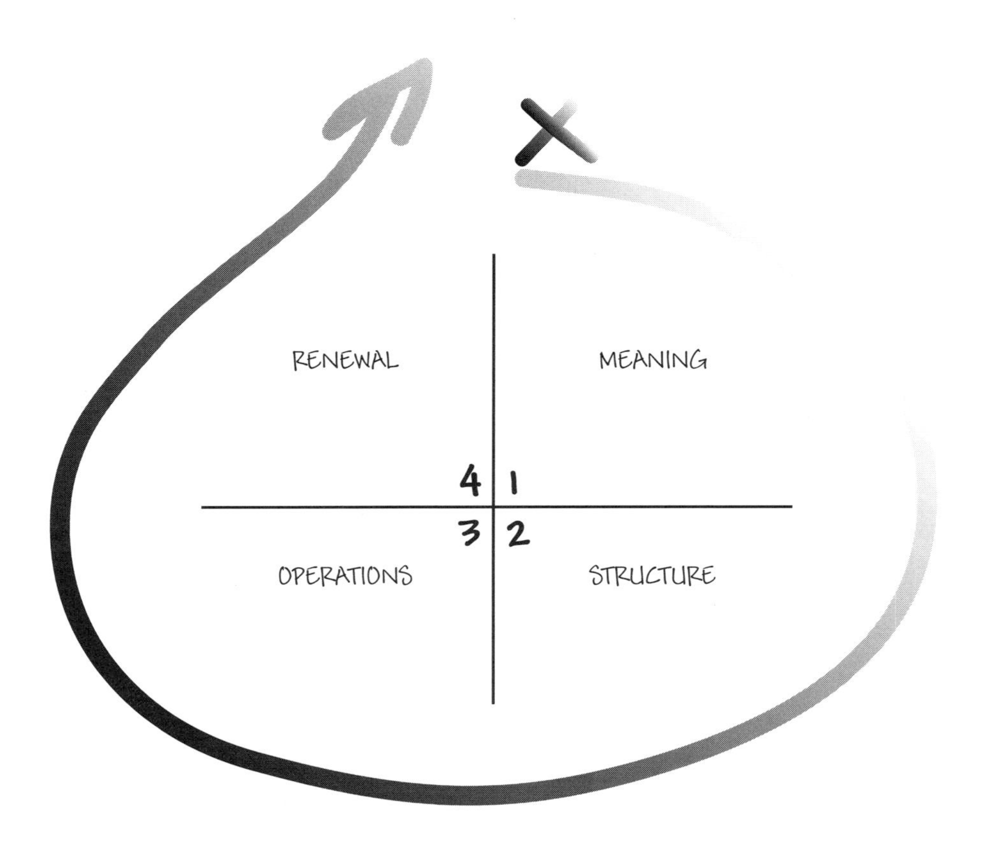

A profile of the learning organization emerged
as one that continues to renew itself –
going through the cycle, moving consciously
from meaning
to structure,
to operations,
to renewal...
and new meaning.

A learning organization
grows from within
as members progressively interiorize
and then manifest
the principles of cycle learning and living,
applying them to major organizational concerns
such as team building,
organizing and planning,
decision making,
and evaluating and reviewing.

Randall K. Murphy, Founder and President of Acclivus Corporation, Dallas, Texas; comments on the use of 4MAT in his organization.

When my colleagues and I were first introduced
to 4MAT twelve years ago,
we were immediately struck by the application
for the work that we do.

We assist client organizations in enabling
and inspiring the performance of their executives and managers,
and their sales, support, and service professionals.
We accomplish this through workshops
and with a variety of support materials
focused on communication, negotiation, planning, and strategy.

Through incorporating the principles of 4MAT
in our instructional design, we have systematically
improved the effectiveness of the learning experiences we create.
And we have measurably increased the results achieved for our clients.

Over the years, as Bernice and her colleagues
have evolved their thinking with regard to 4MAT,
my colleagues and I have evolved our application of 4MAT
to our work.

There is more, though.
We have come to regard 4MAT as a lens
through which to view our process
of working together,
as well as the product of our work.
From the earliest days of our enterprise,
twenty years ago, we have aspired to
a high level of mutual trust, respect, and rapport.
We have placed a high value on collegiality
as a requirement for achieving optimal contribution
from each member of our team.

We have believed, from the beginning,
that intellect, judgment, and creativity —
as well as hard work — prosper in a collegial environment.
While we have always had the right integrity of intent,
we have sometimes lacked the necessary tools.

4MAT has provided us with tools and a methodology
for reaching beyond simply tolerating differences.
Through our increased understanding of learning styles
and our shared commitment to 4MAT,
we have arrived at a point of valuing differences
because of the inherent value of those differences.
In fact, we have developed some adeptness
at utilizing differences and leveraging differences.

From our organizational structure,
to the formation of a project team,
to the plan for a meeting,
to the everyday dialogue between and among colleagues,
we experience the value of differences.
4MAT has helped us accomplish this.
We are not yet (maybe will never be)
perfect practitioners.
We have, though, woven an organizational fabric
that has a rich texture —
neither too smooth nor too rough.
This fabric with its diversity
is proving to be amazingly strong and resilient.

*Acclivus Corporation is a worldwide performance consulting organization.
Acclivus works in partnership with leaders in business and industry
teaching organizations how to build collaborative relationships in order
to achieve optimal results.*

Fine performance comes from
people at all levels
who pay close attention to their environment,
communicate unshakable core values,
and patiently develop the skills
that will enable them
to make sustained contributions to their organizations.
— Tom Peters and Nancy Austin

The 4MAT Organization

Think of the perceiving dimension as it applies to organizations.
Think of the people skills that flow naturally
from the **12 o'clock place,** from sensing and feeling.

Dealing with people realities,
listening intently,
hearing what's really being said,
immersed in the moment,
knowing subjectively,
encompassing the whole,
taking in, being in being,
embedded in experience.
Round and contextual.

The 12 o'clock place is the people place, the experiencing place,
the reality place.

If there is any one "secret" of effectiveness,
it is concentration.
Effective executives do first things first
and they do one thing at a time.

–Peter Drucker

Now think of the product planned,
the final step before the actual doing,
the specified, the chosen,
separate from other possibilities,
the product that comes from the planning
of the **6 o'clock place.**

Examining,
understanding the parts,
planning, connecting to what the world needs.

Objectivity discriminated,
ready for doing, separate and unique.

Sequenced and moving.

The 6 o'clock place is the product planning place.

The leader's goal
is not mere explanation or clarification
but the creation of meaning.
— Warren Bennis

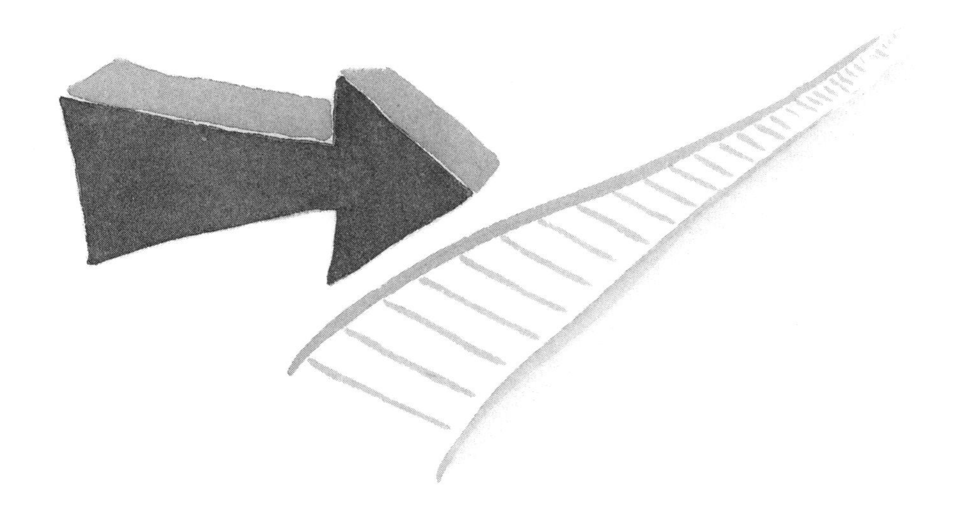

Next think of the processing dimension –
the movement from reflection to action.
What does that mean in an organization?
First think of the necessity for alignment.

Alignment, a word that means
to be together, join with a group, to line up towards.

The "Why" of the company, the mission,
aligned with the whys of the staff and management teams.
Serious time taken with co-workers to dialogue,
to seek necessary affiliations,
the congruence of the "Whys."

Does the mission match the "What" of the company,
the structure that is in place?
Is the vision manifest in the work?
This cannot be accomplished without reflection,
without taking the time from doing to reflect.
If the belief is in the value of dialogue,
does one team or one level make all the major decisions?
If the vision is to create heroes up and down the line,
has the freedom to innovate been actualized?

Alignment is a crucial match of vision and structure,
the Quadrant One and Quadrant Two parts of the cycle.

The **3 o'clock place** is the alignment place.

I soon learned that
there is no "effective personality."
The effective executives I have seen
differ widely in their temperaments
and their abilities, in what they do
and in how they do it,
in their personalities, their knowledge, their interests –
in fact in almost everything that distinguishes human beings.
All they have in common is their ability to get the right things done.
— Peter Drucker

Now think of action moving into high gear,
implementing the plan, doing and redoing, adapting,
the things that naturally flow from the 9 o'clock place.

Are operations congruent with the mission and the structure?
Is the plan being followed?
Are human and capital resources available?
Are there feedback loops
and are they being monitored?
Are actions directed to improving productivity
and enhancing competence?

Action, the doing that is the most visible aspect of an organization,
the Quadrant Three part of the cycle.

The **9 o'clock place** is the action place.

What gets measured gets done.
Measurement is the heart of any improvement process.
It must begin at the outset of the program,
be visible,
and done by the natural work group itself.
—Tom Peters

And finally, the evaluation.
What is the quality of the product?
What can be done to improve it?
What does the data show?
What should be continued?
What should be discontinued?
What should be changed?
What new challenges have emerged?
What new ideas do we have?
What is this product telling us about possible new products?
What shall we do in the future?
Can the organization continue to thrive?

Meeting challenges through renewal,
the Quadrant Four part of the cycle.

Learning to see slow, gradual processes
requires slowing down our frenetic pace
and paying attention to the subtle
as well as the dramatic.
— Peter Senge

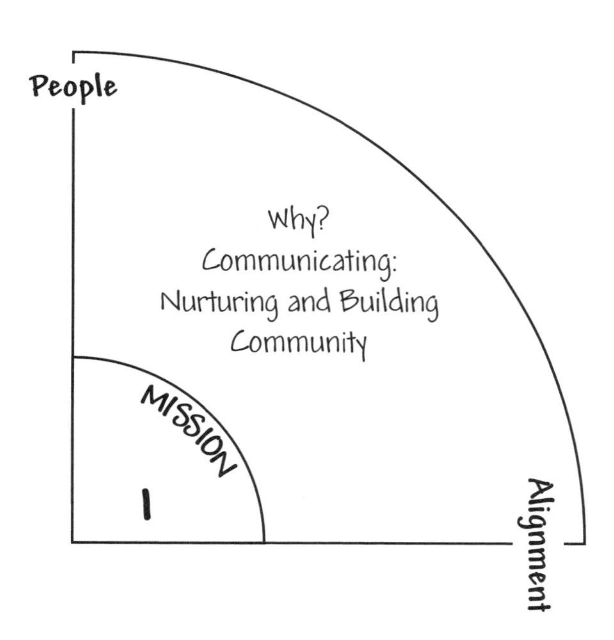

A FURTHER LOOK AT QUADRANT ONE

When we consider **people** at 12 o'clock
and **alignment** at 3 o'clock,
we see how Quadrant One encompasses mission –
the Why? of the organization dialogued and articulated.

The heart of the organizational aspect of Quadrant One
is communication –
the mission understood, embraced and articulated at all levels,
with major attention to articulation from the top levels.

It includes the nurturing and building of community –
nonthreatening environments,
climates of trust and openness,
places to listen, training possibilities,
multiple opportunities for growth,
mentoring.

Forming teams, linking teams together,
asking to listen, not just to ask,
being present to people,
seeing what they see, pondering what they ponder.

Planning for the future
encompasses more than an analytical approach.
Sometime a chart filled with numbers
appears unshakably credible.
It often isn't.
... I prefer to talk about ideas and beliefs instead.
Do my views, my ideas
jibe with where people think the industry is going?
How do our beliefs differ from the analysis?
— John Sculley

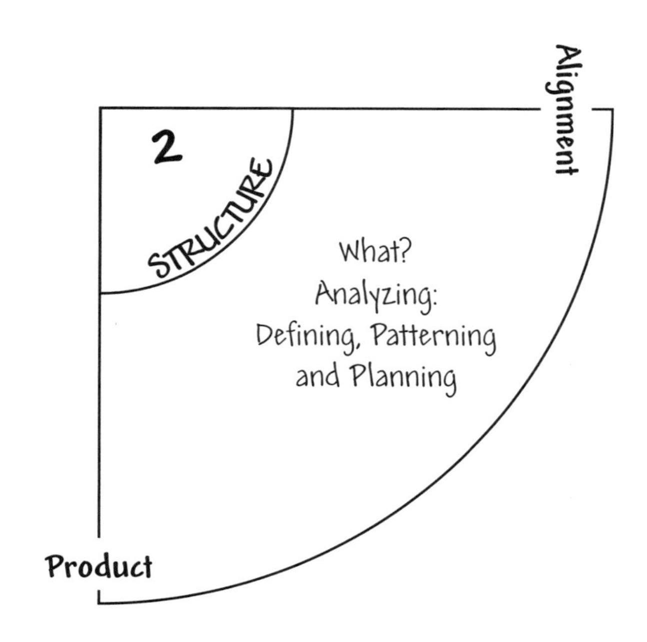

A FURTHER LOOK AT QUADRANT TWO

When we consider **alignment** at 3 o'clock
and **product** at 6 o'clock,
we see how Quadrant Two encompasses structure –
the What? of the organization, the structure,
formed and delineated. Alignment of the mission
with the structure to accomplish that mission.

The heart of the organizational aspect of Quadrant Two
is planning: getting the facts, strategizing, identifying resources,
developing and assigning staff and timelines.

It includes patterning and planning,
deciding the structure that has to be in place for the mission to work,
the patterning of the outside world, the defining of criteria,
gathering the data, examining discrepant events,
attending to myriad details.

Asking the right questions, examining the most salient facts,
lining up the best people, planning for maximum return,
estimating costs and benefits, understanding the whole picture,
imaging the finished product.

The operating talent
carries the institution
toward its objectives,
in the situation, from day to day,
and resolves the issues that arise
as this movement takes place.
This calls for interpersonal skills,
sensitivity to the environment,
tenacity, experience, judgment,
and the ethical soundness,
that the day-to-day movement requires.
Operating is more administering in contrast to leading.
— Robert Greenleaf

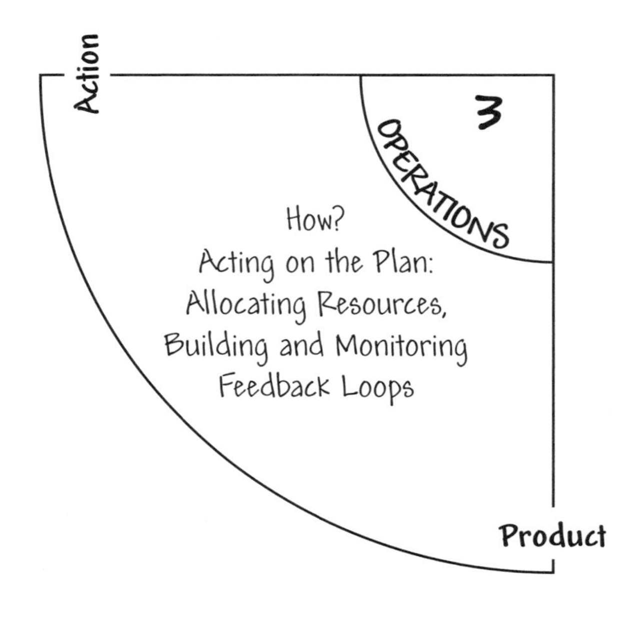

A FURTHER LOOK AT QUADRANT THREE

When we consider **product** at 6 o'clock
and **action** at 9 o'clock,
we see how Quadrant Three encompasses operations –
the How? of the organization, the procedures
prescribed and enacted. The plan put into action.

The heart of the organizational aspect of Quadrant Three
is operations: the mission and plan in action,
acting on the plan, allocating resources,
building and monitoring feedback,
deciding how and when, scheduling with the right sequences,
plan testing, adjustment tinkerings, field testing, reaction listening,
de-buggings.

It includes encouraging and nurturing good tries,
learning from mistakes,
persisting in goal attainment,
knowing which battles to fight and which to concede,
adapting and adjusting.

The Essentials of a Successful Recognition Program

It must be heartfelt.

Along with the necessary big awards for herculean efforts be sure you have the important numerous awards for small acts.

Think systematically about this.

Celebrate what you want to see more of.

— Tom Peters

A FURTHER LOOK AT QUADRANT FOUR

When we consider **action** at 9 o'clock
and **people** at 12 o'clock,
we see how Quadrant Four encompasses
both evaluation and renewal –
the What If? of the organization questioned and evaluated.

The heart of the organizational aspect of Quadrant Four
is evaluation, the rethinking of mission, plan, and operations.
This means renewal, evaluating, editing, challenging,
compromising, pushing boundaries,
thinking in ever-widening circles, celebrating victories.

It includes noting successes,
honoring failures,
reviewing results,
thinking about serendipitous learning,
asking new questions,
creating new forms.

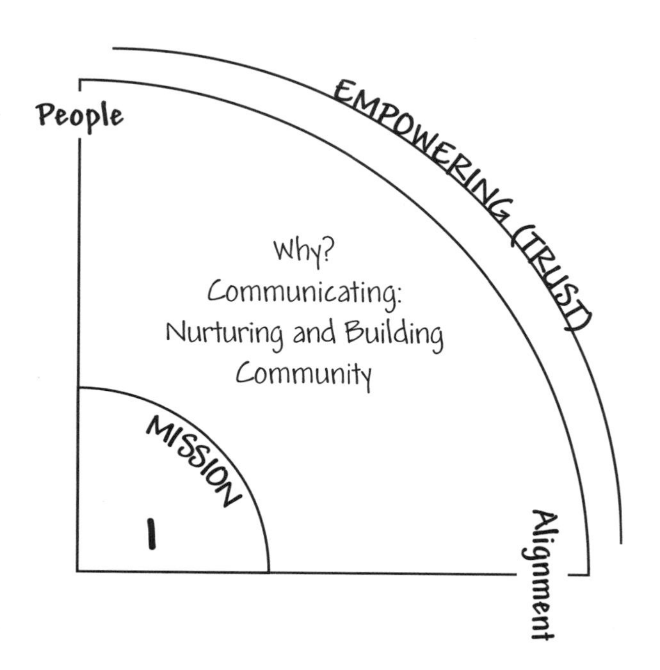
People
EMPOWERING (TRUST)
Why?
Communicating:
Nurturing and Building
Community
MISSION
I
Alignment

Climate for Fostering the Quadrant One Strengths

The ideal outcome in Quadrant One
is a climate of trust,
the kind of trust that permits authentic communications.

The way to achieve such a climate
is to be trustworthy yourself,
to honor diversity,
to listen well,
to speak honestly,
to play fair,
to seek the common good.

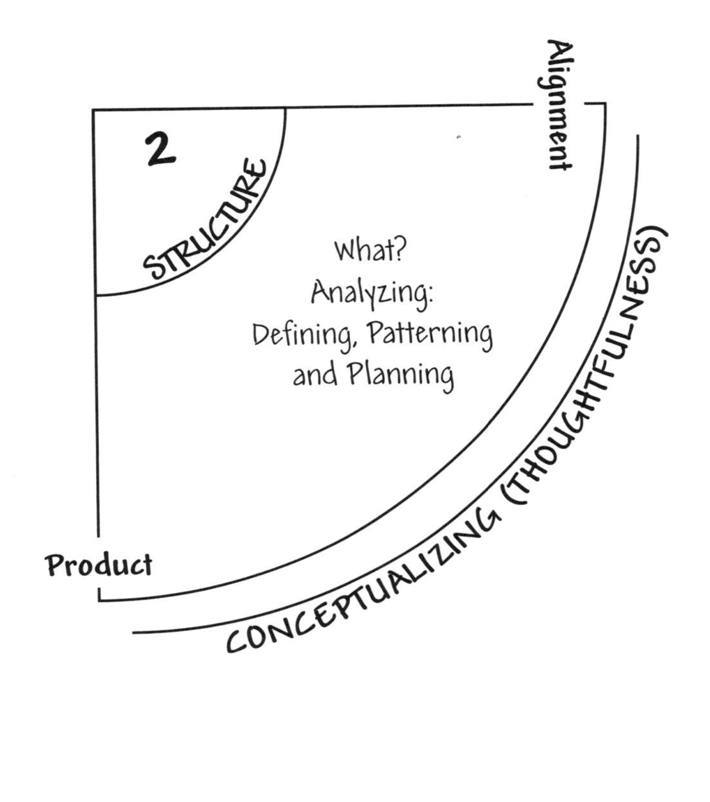
2
STRUCTURE
What?
Analyzing:
Defining, Patterning
and Planning
Alignment
Product
CONCEPTUALIZING (THOUGHTFULNESS)

Climate for Fostering the Quadrant Two Strengths
The ideal outcome in Quadrant Two
is a climate of thoughtfulness,
the kind of thoughtfulness that is open to dialogue
and ponders and questions its own ideas.

The way to achieve that climate is to model conceptual thinking,
to confront the unknown,
to seek answers to tough questions,
to value research,
to use the parts to understand the whole,
to acknowledge that no one knows it all.

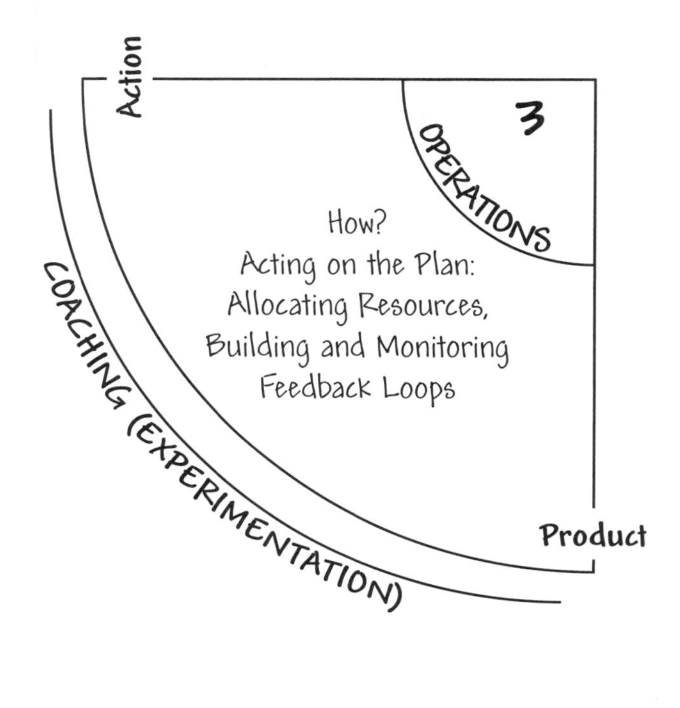
Action
3
OPERATIONS
How?
Acting on the Plan:
Allocating Resources,
Building and Monitoring
Feedback Loops
COACHING (EXPERIMENTATION)
Product

Climate for Fostering the Quadrant Three Strengths

The ideal outcome in Quadrant Three
is a climate of experimentation,
the kind of experimentation that leads to creative expression.

The way to achieve such a climate
is to act with confidence
and the courage to risk failure,
to make decisions
and be prepared to deal with the consequences,
to devise contingency plans,
to establish and maintain mentoring,
to be flexible,
to deal wisely with feedback.

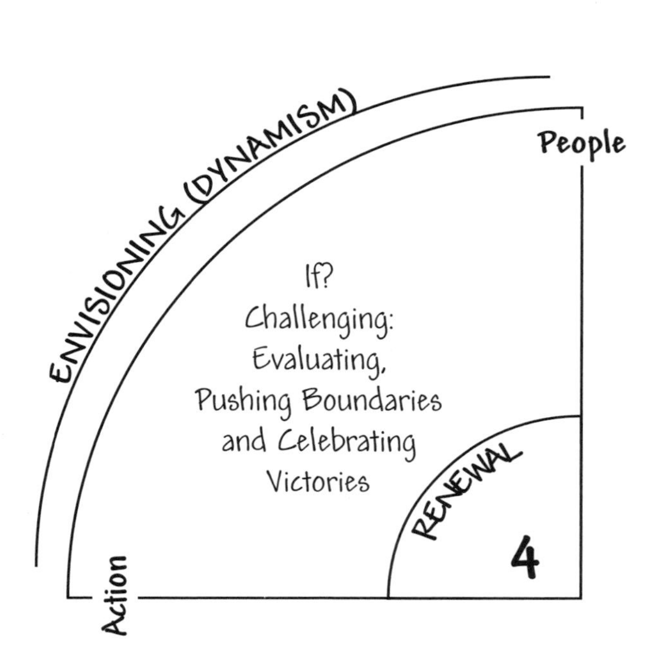
ENVISIONING (DYNAMISM)
People
If?
Challenging:
Evaluating,
Pushing Boundaries
and Celebrating
Victories
RENEWAL
4
Action

Climate for Fostering the Quadrant Four Strengths

The ideal outcome in Quadrant Four
is a climate of dynamism,
a work culture that supports innovation
and thinking in ever-widening circles.

The way to achieve such a climate
is to be willing to be wrong,
to handle surprise well,
to give and take honest criticism,
to learn from the past,
to acknowledge success,
to share the credit,
to laugh with one's peers,
and to face the future with renewed vision
and with courage.

I believe the lower half of the cycle,
the Analyzing
and
the Acting on the plan,
is what Management entails.

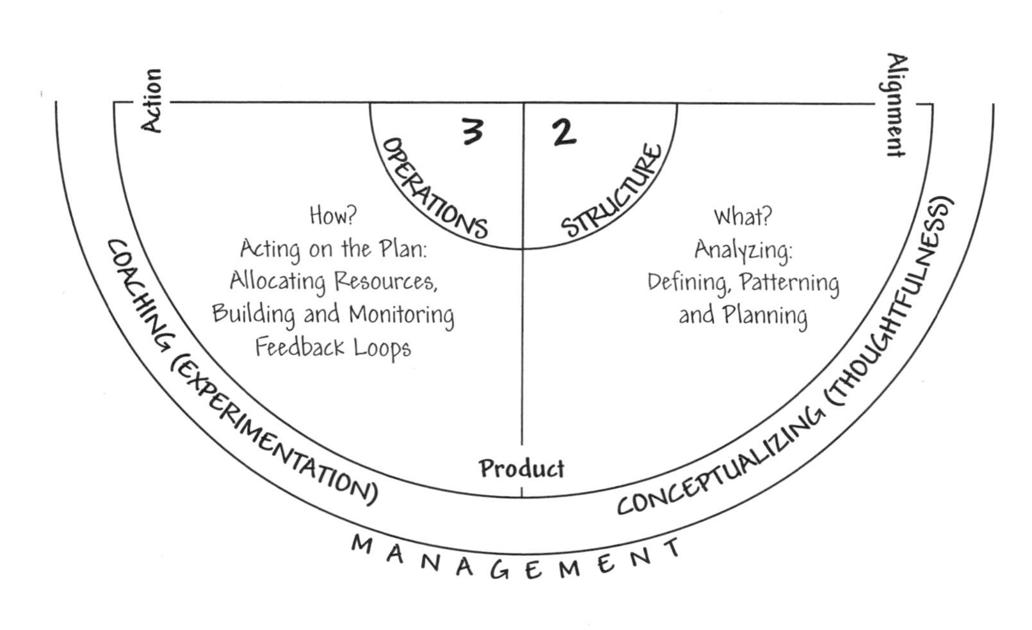

I believe the upper half of the cycle,
the Communicating
and
the Challenging,
is what Leadership entails.

Warren Bennis and Tom Peters
talk a lot about the tasks
that fall in the upper half of the cycle.
Perhaps this is because they,
like so many of us,
have found it lacking
in so many organizations.

We need to do it all.

The leader as artist
will rely on
images as well as memos,
poetry as well as policy,
reflection as well as command,
and reframing as well as refitting.
— Terrence Deal

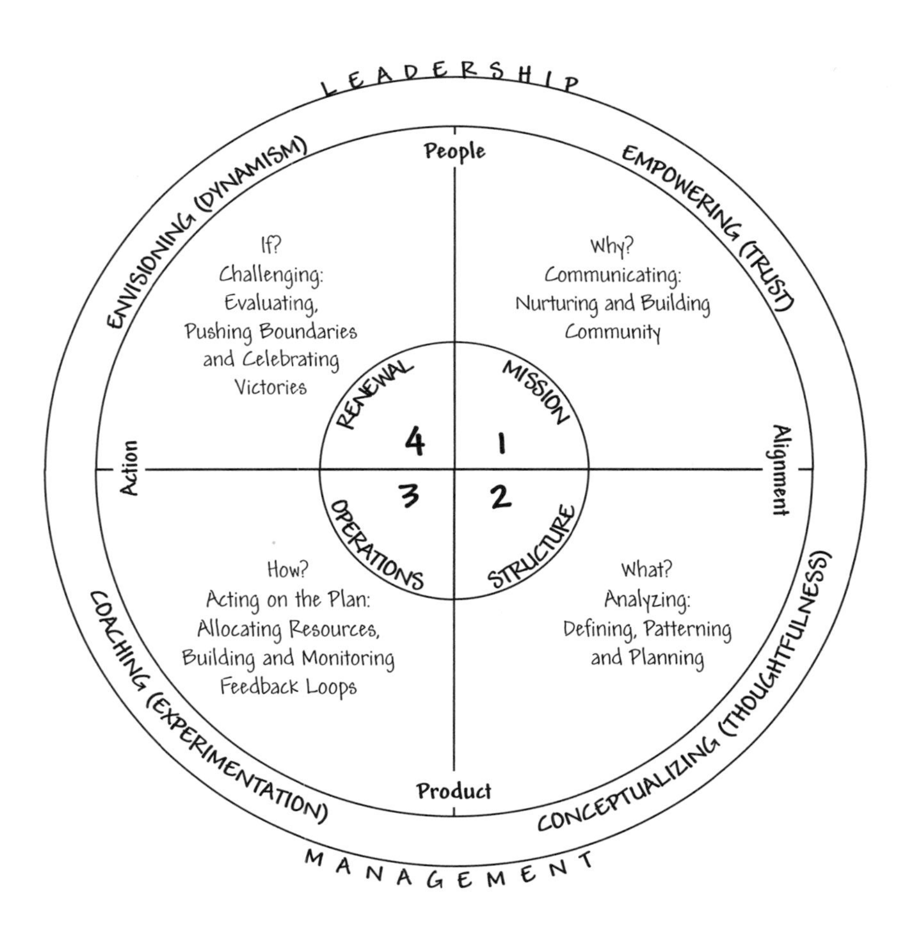
LEADERSHIP
People
ENVISIONING (DYNAMISM)
EMPOWERING (TRUST)
If?
Challenging:
Evaluating,
Pushing Boundaries
and Celebrating
Victories
Why?
Communicating:
Nurturing and Building
Community
RENEWAL
MISSION
4
1
Action
Alignment
3
2
OPERATIONS
STRUCTURE
How?
Acting on the Plan:
Allocating Resources,
Building and Monitoring
Feedback Loops
What?
Analyzing:
Defining, Patterning
and Planning
COACHING (EXPERIMENTATION)
CONCEPTUALIZING (THOUGHTFULNESS)
Product
MANAGEMENT

An organization without the balance
of all four quadrants
is by design
an organization in conflict.
— Ulf Caap, IKEA, North America

The truly effective manager and leader
will need multiple tools,
the skill to use each of them,
and the wisdom to
match frames to situations.
— Terrence Deal

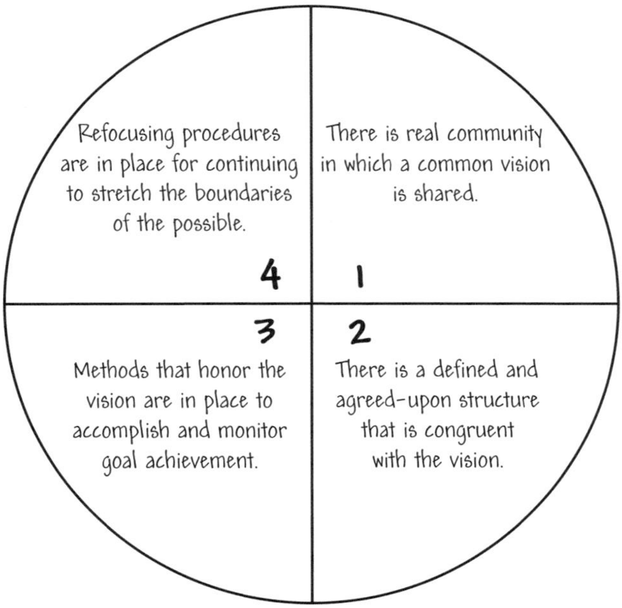

The 4MAT Cycle is a framework
for balance and wholeness:

Community,
Structure,
Operations,
Renewal –
all vital attributes in a process
of ongoing improvement and innovation
and productivity, competence and power.

Management applications of 4MAT
are included in Appendix B, page 439.

As a leader
one must have facility
in tempting the hearer
into that leap of imagination
that connects the verbal concept
to the hearer's own experience.
The limitation on language,
to the communicator,
*is that the **hearer** must make that leap of imagination.*
One of the arts of communicating is to say just enough
to facilitate that leap.
— Robert Greenleaf

LEADING

Leadership styles bear definite relationships
to learning styles.

But the results of our leadership surveys
indicate that the situation the leader is in
is a crucial indicator of effective leader behavior.
For example, if I take over
the management of a growing business
and discover my predecessor was strongly disliked
and her strategy was to divide and conquer,
I need to go to my Quadrant One strengths
to begin to build the trust with the staff
that will be necessary for a productive learning climate.

If the structure of operations were in disarray,
I would need to go to my Quadrant Two
planning and organizing skills
in order to begin to correct that situation.

In other words, leaders, like learners, need
to function with some degree of comfort in all four quadrants.

All four quadrants are vital to the health of any organization.
Leaders need to move around the cycle
and model that movement for others.

Leaders need to make diverse gifts productive,
(their own as well as those of others).
Unique, personal achievements
need to enhance the organization's competence and productivity.

TYPE ONE LEADER

Is empowering and involved.
Seeks alignment between personal and organizational values.
Relies primarily on consensus and support in decision making.
Judges others by how they treat people.
Expects people to grow in self-awareness.
Is a good communicator but sometimes
focuses on feelings at the expense of the message.

Works well with supportive staff who share the sense of mission.
Tackles problems by first verifying perceptions
and possible solutions with others.

Has difficulty tolerating inconsiderate people.
Experiences inner conflict when the organization's
behavior/structure is in conflict with its values.

Works to enhance organizational solidarity.
Creates a sense of community.
Exercises authority with trust and participation.
Leads by articulating and acting on the mission.
Thrives on developing good ideas.
Relies on group values as primary structure.

Communication strength is active listening.

TYPE TWO LEADER

Is problem-focused and lively-minded.
Seeks alignment between people and procedures.
Relies primarily on data for decision making.
Judges others by their accomplishments.
Expects people to seek increasing professional knowledge.
Is reluctant to speak until all the facts are known,
which often causes communication problems.

Works well with staff who follow through,
are well organized, and have things down on paper.

Tackles problems with logic and rationality.
Has difficulty tolerating action without rational bases.
Strives for perfection which, coupled with fear of failure,
causes inner conflict.

Works to enhance organization's reputation for prestige.
Creates a solid organizational structure.
Exercises authority with assertive persuasion.
Leads by honoring and implementing principles and procedures.
Thrives on understanding and working through complex problems.
Relies on organized planning.
Needs others to provide impetus.

Communication strength is precision in words and data.

TYPE THREE LEADER

Is productive and action-oriented.
Seeks alignment between goals and output.
Relies primarily on results for decision making.
Judges others by their straightforwardness and hard work.
Expects people to seek increasing competence.
Often has communication difficulties
because of a straightforward manner
that tends to overlook people's feelings.

Works well with staff who are task-oriented and move quickly.
Tackles problems with immediacy, often without consulting others.
Has difficulty tolerating indecisiveness.
Is strongly task-oriented which may confound others who are
strongly oriented to people concerns.

Works to enhance organization's productivity and solvency.
Creates a productive climate, often pitching in and working
side-by-side with co-workers.

Exercises authority by demanding bottom-line results.
Leads by personal forcefulness, inspiring quality.
Thrives on solving difficult problems.
Relies on efficiency of output.
Needs others to provide team leadership.

Communication strength is directness.

TYPE FOUR LEADER

Is dynamic and enthusiastic.
Seeks alignment between what is and what might be.
Relies primarily on intuition for decision making.
Judges others by their enthusiasm, their liveliness.
Expects people to see new possibilities as they act on their work.
Often communicates poorly because of expectations
that people should know what to do and a preoccupation with
the present that leads to forgetfulness of past communications.

Works well with staff who are quick, both in thought and action,
and who can follow up and implement details.

Tackles problems by intuiting possibilities and taking risks.
Has difficulty tolerating people who do not see
what needs to be done.
Is flexible and open, yet firmly set in deeply held values,
which causes inner conflict.

Works to enhance organization's reputation as a front runner.
Creates opportunities.
Exercises authority by holding up a vision of what might be.
Leads by energizing people.
Thrives on change.
Focuses on organizational vision.
Needs others to provide details and follow-through.

Communication strength is articulating the big picture.

Stretching Exercise

Fours

- Try to focus on structure.
- Take some time to reflect before acting.
- Show some care for systems and procedures.
- Spend some time on what to do.
- Think strategically.
- Appreciate that others have a low tolerance for chaos.
- Develop a model to structure your insights.
- Communicate your thinking process.
- Choose what risks to take.
- Challenge disorganization.

Ones

- Try to focus on procedures and specific outcomes.
- Act more quickly.
- Share some of your thoughts as well as your feelings.
- Spend some time on how to do it.
- Make ideas workable.
- Spend some time planning.
- Deal with conflict.
- Try new things.
- Look at the bottom line.
- Challenge lack of closure.

Threes

- Take some time to chat with people about what is going on.
- Take time to honor the process.
- Try sharing your feelings with others.
- Care for other people's needs.
- Look for the values in ideas.
- Try to consider that other ideas may be possible before coming to closure.
- Imagine.
- Take the time to allow others to find their own meaning.
- Weigh alternative possibilities.
- Challenge action for its own sake.

Twos

- Try some action before you have a perfect plan.
- Take some risks.
- Try being open to change.
- Go with your instincts.
- Try sharing your questions with others.
- Be outgoing. Approach people you don't know.
- Open your mind to other possibilities.
- Dare to experience chaos.
- Try to inspire others.
- Challenge complacency.

Stretching Exercise

Self-renewing leaders strive to understand their strengths.
They look at where they need to grow.
They also move into areas that are not as compatible
with their unique style
in order to energize themselves,
in order to be lifelong learners.

The lists on the facing page
detail the main areas for growth in each style.

For example, if you favor Oneness as a leader,
in order to achieve more balance
you would need to work on
the items listed in Quadrant One.

These are things that take more energy,
that the leader needs to work harder to achieve.
They are the things for stretching,
the things that lead to wholeness,
both for a leader and for an organization.

Mentoring Around the Circle

The Learner

- Shifting
- Risking
- Intuiting
- Collaborating
- Modifying
- Adapting
- Persisting
- Acting

The Leader

- Enlarging diffusion networks
- Promoting
- Championing
- Getting resources
- Energizing
- Tolerating failure
- Reforming teams
- Letting the leaders emerge from the tasks
- Facilitating "independence"

The Leader

- Capturing enthusiasm
- Motivating, Witnessing
- Acclimating
- Facilitating
- Supporting, Interacting
- Staying in touch
- Valuing, Nurturing
- Creating meaning: symbols, rituals, myths
- Transmitting significant values

The Learner

- Receiving
- Being acted upon

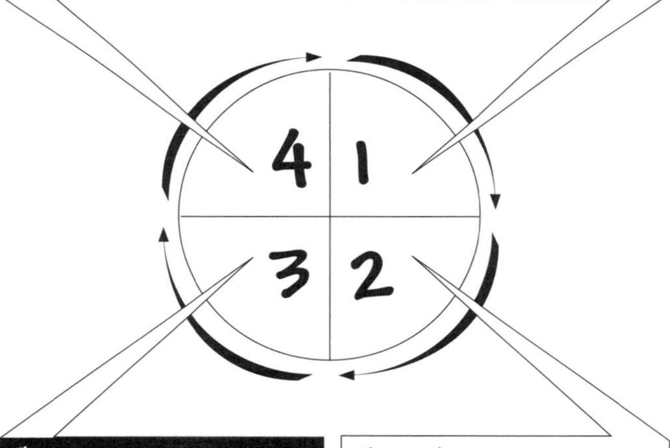

The Learner

- Risking
- Examining
- Trying/failing
- Testing
- Improvising
- Fixing things
- Tinkering

The Leader

- Setting up environments and attitudes that encourage experimentation
- Sponsoring, nurturing good tries, generating opportunities, leading cheers, coaching (quietly guiding the diffusion process)
- Reinforcing the "right" answers

The Leader

- Analyzing
- Theorizing
- Defining
- Organizing
- Planning
- Coordinating
- Conceptualizing
- Pattern Making
- Teaching
- Asking the "right" questions

The Learner

- Conceptualizing
- Interacting

Leaders as Mentors

To be a leader is to set the climate –
to mentor,
to form the structure,
to operationalize plans,
to create space, clearings
where people can grow.

The leader's tasks shift
as the cycle evolves –
from motivating,
to planning,
to operationalizing,
to promoting.

Beginning with capturing enthusiasm,
culminating in facilitating independence –
letting multiple leaders emerge from the tasks,
regrouping as tasks shift.

From center stage to the wings,
from the field to the sidelines,
and all the while
the spokesperson for the mission,
the servant to the process.

The image of firm control
and crisp rationality
often attributed to managers
has little relevance to the messy world
of complexity, conflict, and uncertainty
that they typically inhabit.
They need multiple frames to survive.
— Terrence Deal

Is there any other way to maintain
serenity in the face of uncertainty?
One follows the steps of the creative process
which require that one stay with
conscious analysis as far as it will carry one,
and then withdraw,
release the analytical pressure,
if only for a moment, in full confidence
that a resolving insight will come.
— Robert Greenleaf

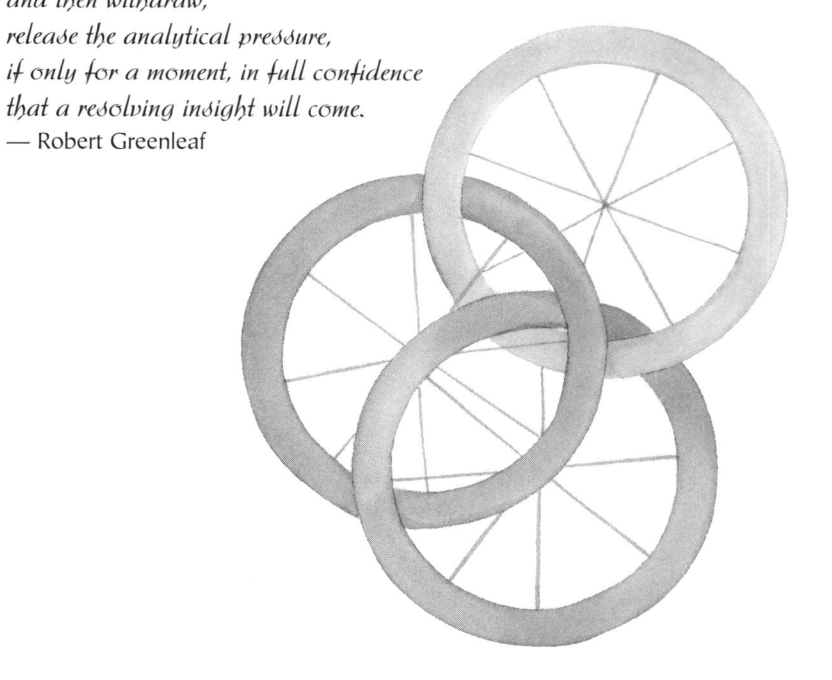

Problem Solving with 4MAT

When we are asked to solve a problem,
most of the time we assume we know what the problem is.

We zero right into Quadrant Three,
"What do I need to do to fix this problem?"

The truth of the matter is that most of the time
the core of the problem is not what it first appears to be.
Our perceptions influence what we see.
The same problem appears differently to different eyes.
The theories we develop and carry with us
(our means of creating order out of all that surrounds us)
color our ability to see what is important and what is not.
We try to solve what we think the problem is
and often miss the real problem.

If I use the cycle to problem solve, instead of beginning with
"How do I solve this problem?" (Quadrant Three),
I begin by defining the What of the problem (Quadrant Two).
I then ask, "Why is this occurring?
Why has this surfaced?" (Quadrant One).
Instead of first attempting to solve the problem,
I begin the task of defining it
by asking why I have this problem at all.
The Why leads to the What and then, much more realistically,
to the How of the solution.
If I follow with a Quadrant Four question,
"What consequence will I have if I implement this new solution?"
I will have completed the cycle,
very likely with far more productive results.

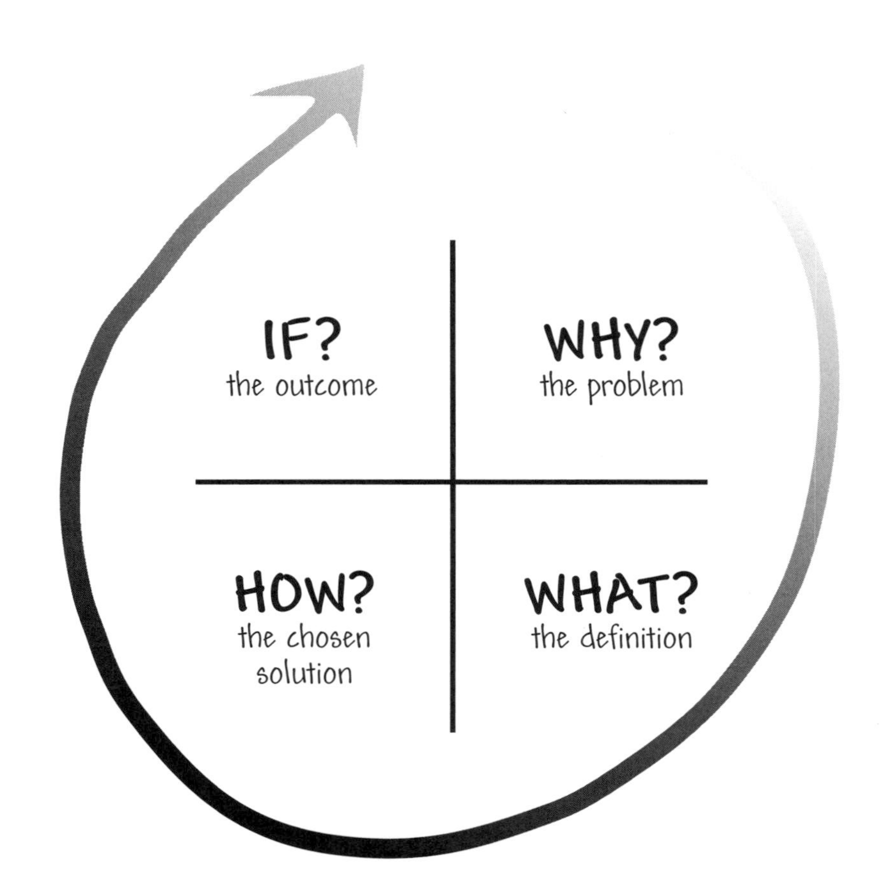

It is in the formulation of the problem
that individuality is expressed,
that creativity is stimulated,
that nuances and subtleties are discovered.
— Herbert Thelen

The Why of a problem directs the way
to problem definition.

The trick is to get to the Why,
which is always a deeper issue.

Instead of rushing to judgment on What the problem is,
taking the time to develop the Why of the situation
honors the intuitive, subjective evidence.

And after the solution is chosen,
we can call again upon the subjective, the intuitive,
looking at the Quadrant Four aspect and asking –
If we do this, what then?
What will this solution create?

The Learning Style exercise had a tremendous effect on me,
forcing me to take stock of my problem-solving pattern…
My instincts are often very good, and I'm just as likely to make
the right decision as not, based on my experience.
What frightens me is my apparent inability
to try out other problem-solving techniques.
— Social Worker as quoted by David Kolb.

Most of us need to expand
our repertoire of problem-solving techniques,
working through the questions in all four quadrants,
becoming aware of those we tend to favor
and those we tend to neglect.

The upper half of the cycle,
the most often neglected part,
is crucial
for successful problem solving.

We need to learn how to use other methods
besides our own favorite approaches
if we are to become skilled problem solvers.

Framing a problem through each of the four quadrants brings

Q 1: insight, imagination, subjectivity, shared expertise –

Q 2: relevant variables, data analysis, alternatives, planning –

Q 3: common sense choices, intuitive synthesis of evidence, action –

Q 4: feedback, interpretation, refinement, closure and rethinking.

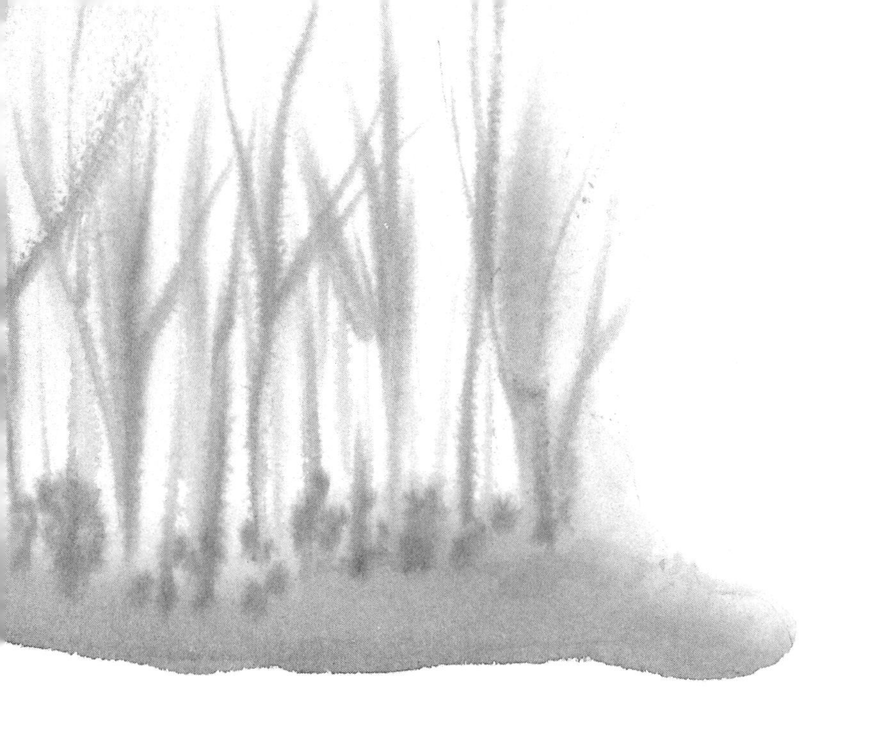

The effective decision maker
always assumes that the event
that clamors for his/her attention
is in reality a symptom.

[S/he] looks for the true problem…
not content with doctoring the symptom alone.
— Peter Drucker

Decision Making with 4MAT

Just as we confront problems regularly,
so we face decisions every day of our lives.
Some are easy, some are difficult.
With the difficult ones the hardest part is
acknowledging that a decision has to be made.
We prefer to put it off, to ignore impending conflict,
to look away from what is and pretend it is not,
to resist what is rapidly becoming obvious because it poses difficulty.

As with problems,
the Why of decisions is often not readily apparent.
Symptoms are disguised.

"My back hurts; it must be a physical problem," rather than,
perhaps dealing with my unexpressed anger.

"My secretary is just not of the caliber I need,"
rather than
"My directives are often confusing and rushed."

"My husband is not a feeling person," rather than
"My continual carping makes quiet, reflective
discussions nearly impossible."

"My employees don't participate enough
in the decision-making process," rather than
"I need to make sure the climate
I create encourages such behavior."

Discover the Why of the decision and the most difficult work is done.

Human beings are activities –
it is not the doing humans do,
but the doing humans are.
— Robert Kegan

Once the discovery is made
and the desire to change becomes a commitment,
then the tasks of examining alternatives,
analyzing the pluses and minuses,
choosing among costs,
winnowing for efficiency and for elegance,
and anticipating possible outcomes
flow around the cycle.

Choices are made and implemented.

And this is followed then by new decisions
that have to be made in light of what has been.

The cycle renews.

Our deeds follow us.
What we do
is what we are.

Achievement is a we thing,
not a me thing,
always the product
of many heads and hands.
— J. Atkinson

Teaming with 4MAT

Individuals may stretch for years
to achieve balance within themselves.

In forming teams
we have the opportunity to seek in groups
the balance
of oneness, twoness, threeness, and fourness.

People with high interpersonal and intrapersonal
processing and brainstorming skills (Ones),
plus those with the ability to conceptualize
and create models (Twos),
and those whose strength is to make things happen,
to operationalize a task (Threes),
and those who are risk takers,
boundary breakers, open-ended thinkers (Fours),
are all needed to achieve excellence.

Their very diversity brings strength to teams.

Two are better than one,
because they have a good reward for their toil.
For if they fall,
one will lift up his fellow;
woe to him who is alone when he falls
and has not another to lift him up.
Again, if two lie together, they are warm;
but how can one be warm alone?
And though a man might prevail against one who is alone,
two will withstand him.
A threefold cord is not quickly broken.
— Holy Bible, Ecclesiastes 4:9-13

In our seminars we invite team members
to trace their learning survey profiles
on transparent film.
These profiles indicate their preferences and strengths
as learners and leaders.
Then they overlay their individual graphs with those of others
and examine the team's balance or lack of balance.

We ask participants to comment on what they see.
They are usually honest and open about the strengths and the gaps.

When there is a noticeable lack of balance
(no Ones or Twos on the team, for example),
I ask team members how they accomplish the tasks
that typically fall within the underrepresented quadrant.

Their answers (usually with much laughter) are:
"With difficulty,"
"We take turns in doing those things,"
"We save them up until we are forced to do them."

It appears the gap is well known to them.

Science is rooted in conversations.
— Werner Heisenberg

... A unique relationship develops among team members who enter into dialogue regularly. They develop a deep trust that cannot help but carry over to discussions. They develop a richer understanding of the uniqueness of each person's point of view.
— Peter Senge

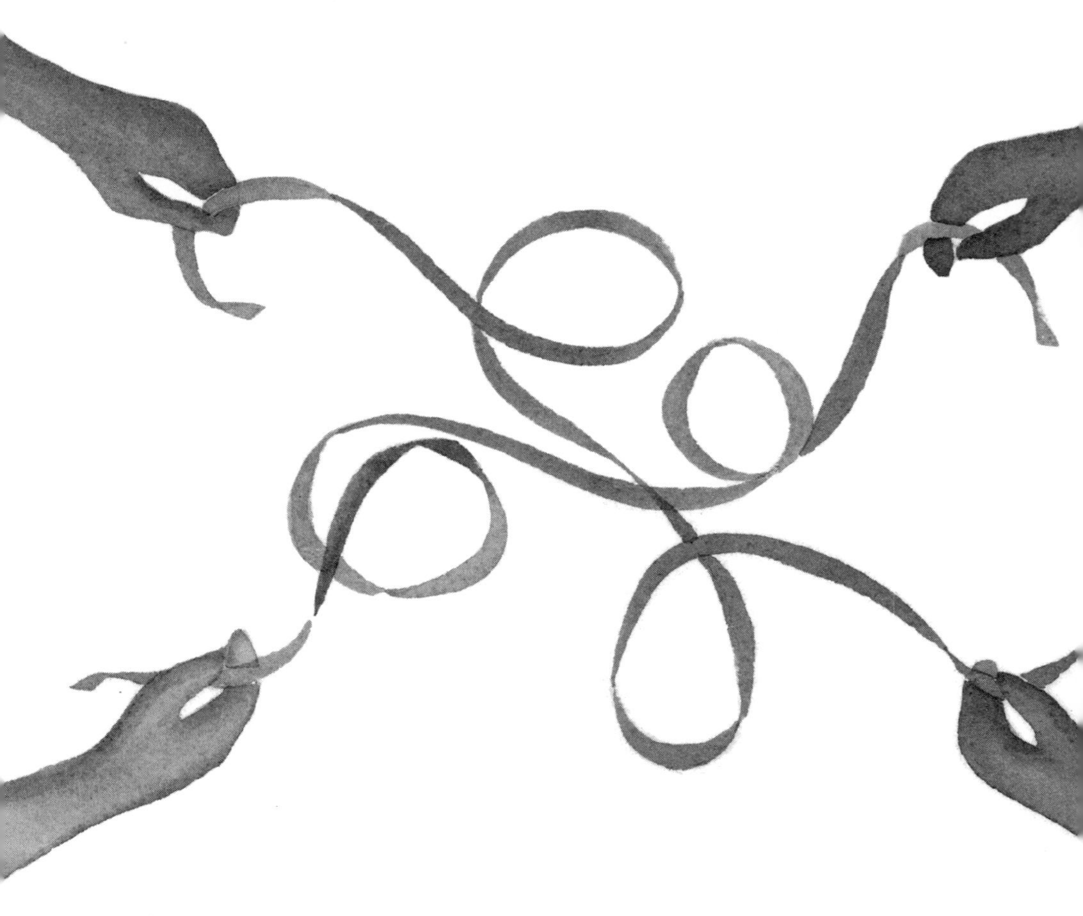

When we draw attention
to the strengths of individual team members
and acknowledge any lack of balance in the group,
then the team can see itself
and function more as a whole,
finding ways to fill in the gaps
and strive towards balance.

Acknowledging that we need each other
makes a great difference to the success of the team process.
One of the most powerful variables in learning
is the interdependence and the interaction of team members.

Understanding and operating
from the premise
that individuals favor certain places on the cycle,
places where they are particularly graceful,
fosters a team spirit that nurtures the wholeness necessary
for problem solving,
decision making
and successful implementation.

Real dialogue is where two or more people
become willing
to suspend their certainty in each other's presence.
— David Bohm

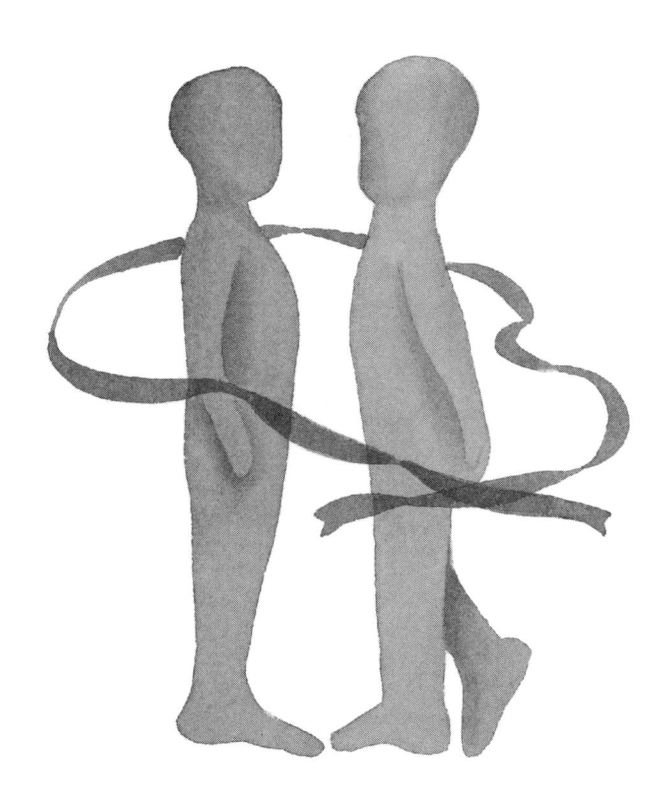

Meeting with 4MAT

To reach people,
to understand them,
to walk in their shoes and share their dreams,
to celebrate their gifts,
not just showcase our own –
these things are the motivating forces of effective communication
and fruitful meetings.

Understanding 4MAT aids effective communication.
Knowing where people are most comfortable
helps us to listen.
Understanding the approaches
that will both comfort and stretch people
is a powerful tool,
especially when used with kindness and courtesy.

Practicing the art of real dialogue is essential.
Honoring, even celebrating, the differences in others
as gifts for our own learning
is a major goal of good communication.
The result is personal mastery and lifelong learning.

To live the cycle
is to improve the ability to communicate well.

In the high-value enterprise,
only one asset grows more valuable
as it is used:
the problem solving, identifying
and brokering skills of key people.
—Robert B. Reich

Examine the process
for conducting a successful meeting.

Purpose:	Why are we having this meeting?
Problem:	What are the goals?
Process:	How will the meeting be structured to attain these goals?
Outcome:	If these goals are implemented, what possible new decisions will we have to make? Are we ready to do that at this time?

There are certain characteristics of meetings
that are painful for people of any learning style.

There are, as well, certain strategies that make meetings
fruitful for people of any certain learning style.

All of us have some difficulty
in some parts of most meetings.

It would be prudent, when possible,
to include in all important meetings
the strategies that lead to success.

CHARACTERISTICS FOR TYPE ONES

Painful Meetings	Successful Meetings
• The Leader is insensitive to feelings.	• Connections are made.
• There is a lack of trust among the group.	• Honesty is encouraged.
• There are unresolved conflicts.	• Interests are elicited.
• Consideration is not given to people who will be affected by the group's decision.	• Time is allowed for discussion about feelings.
• The meeting has no personal relevance.	• The group leader provides for consensus building.

CHARACTERISTICS FOR TYPE TWOS

Painful Meetings	Successful Meetings
• There is no agenda.	• Issues and tasks are clearly defined.
• The Leader does not understand the total picture.	• Information is based on facts.
• There is no time for preparation.	• There is adequate notice for preparation.
• There is insufficient time spent defining the problem.	• Pros and cons are weighed.
• No clarity is achieved as meeting progresses.	• The group stays on task.
• There is insufficient information for problem-solving.	• There is an objective perspective.

CHARACTERISTICS FOR TYPE THREES

Painful Meetings	Successful Meetings
• There is a lack of focus, forays into side issues.	• There is a productive, problem-solving climate.
• Emotions are vented.	• Common sense is elicited.
• Personalities are dealt with, not issues.	• Ideas are used.
• There is inattention to practical realities.	• Decisions are aligned with the realities of existing structures and resources.
• The Leader does not move to closure.	• Closure is achieved.

CHARACTERISTICS FOR TYPE FOURS

Painful Meetings	Successful Meetings
• There is a rigid adherence to agenda and/or timetable.	• There is a flexible agenda.
• People are tentative and cautious.	• The participants look beyond stated objectives.
• Strong, spirited interactions are not welcome.	• Energy is generated.
• There are long monologues.	• Actions are based on intuition.
• There is only pretense at discussion, because in reality decisions already have been made.	• Talk of possible creative action is encouraged.

Components of Successful Meetings

THE PROCESS...

PURPOSE

1

WHY?

- Invite the right people.
- Create climate of trust.
- Communicate purpose clearly.
- Determine right number of people to accomplish task.
- Take time to explore what each individual already knows and feels.

PROBLEM

2

WHAT?

- Define task or problem.
- Discuss the known facts.
- Exchange all ideas and information.
- Decide if research is needed.

PROCESS

3

HOW?

- Assign roles: facilitator, recorder.
- Work from a prioritized agenda with time constraints.
- Consider alternatives.
- Choose plan.
- Establish feedback loops.
- Reach closure.
- Summarize with timelines.
- Record.

OUTCOME

4

IF?

- Give assignments for next meeting.
- Schedule feedback reports on progress of actions/ solutions taken.
- Acknowledge work accomplished.

What we call the beginning is often the end.
And to make an end is to make a beginning.
The end is where we start from.

We shall not cease from exploration
And the end of all our exploring
Will be to arrive where we started
And to know the place for the first time.
— T.S. Eliot

The cycle is old.
The cycle is evident in many places.

Humans have been learning this way for a long time.

We always begin with meaning
and in the end come back to ourselves,
to speak in our own voice.

I have chosen a few examples from management researchers
to illustrate the naturalness of the cycle.

The following are taken from
Michael Fullan on Change,
Terrence Deal and Lee Bolman on Corporate Culture,
Ned Herrmann on Creativity,
Donald Norman on Action Stages,
Proctor and Gamble on Project Stages,
and Warren Bennis on Strategic Planning.

Management applications of 4MAT
are included in Appendix B, page 439.

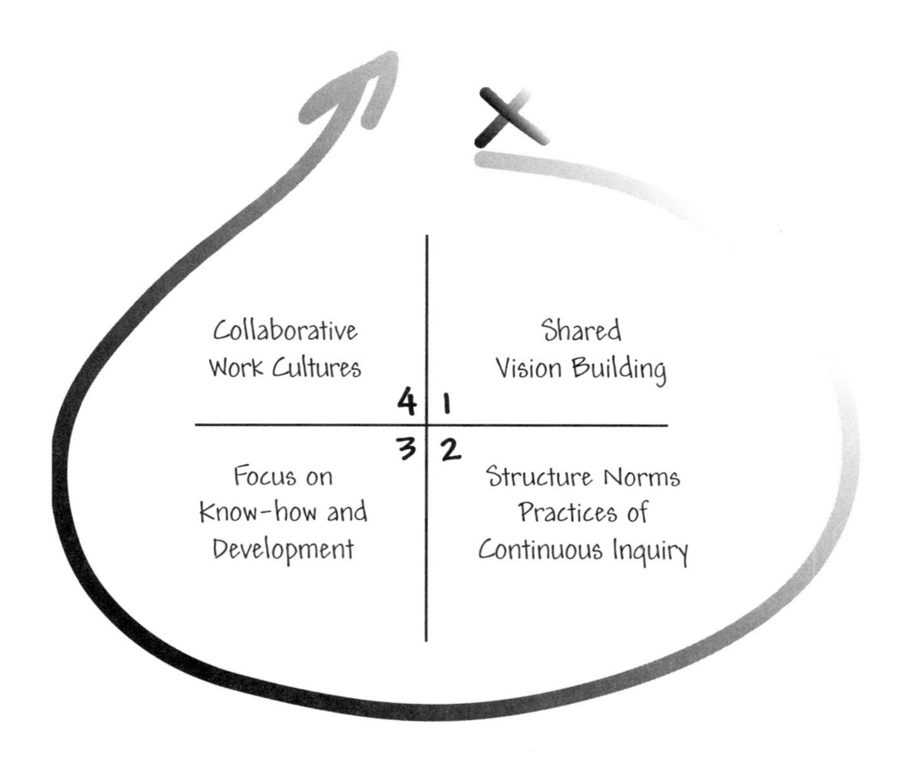

Michael Fullan

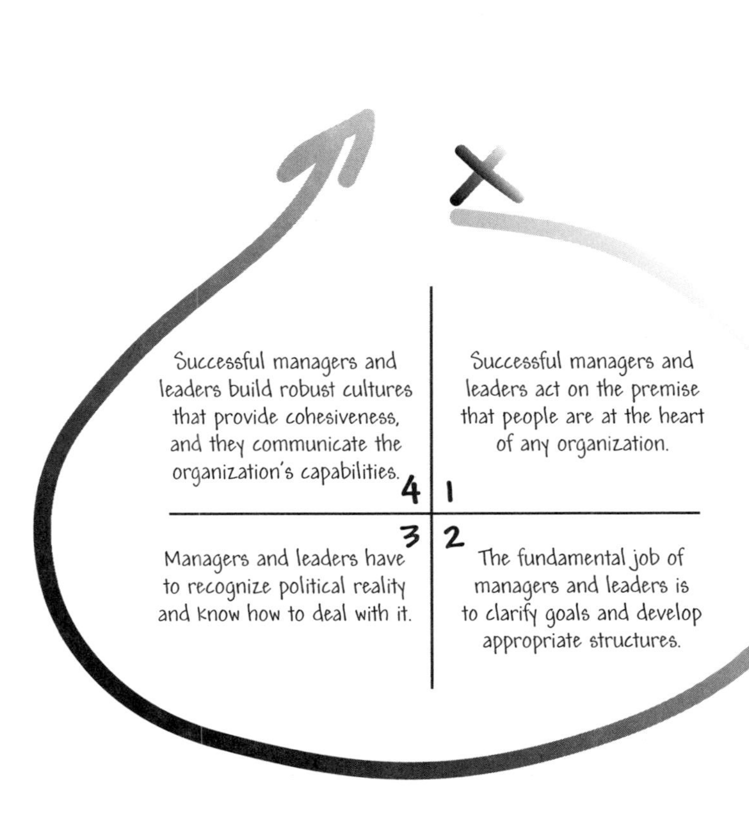

Terrence Deal and Lee Bolman

Seven Stages of Action
Forming the goal
Forming the intention
Specifying an action
Executing the action
Perceiving the state of the world
(what's happening with/in the action)
Interpreting the state of the world
Evaluating the outcome

Donald Norman

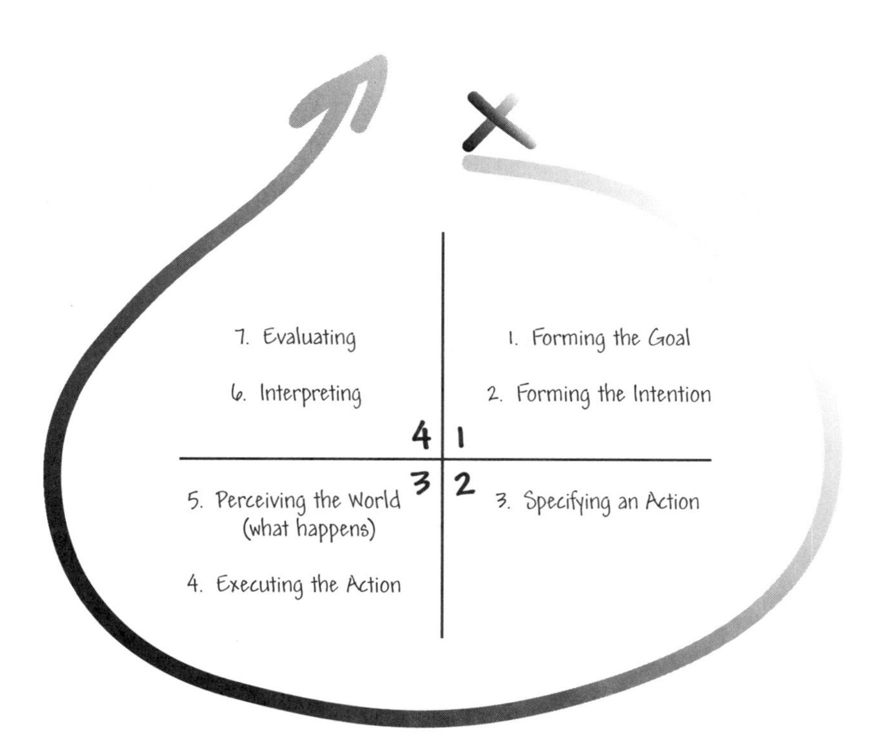

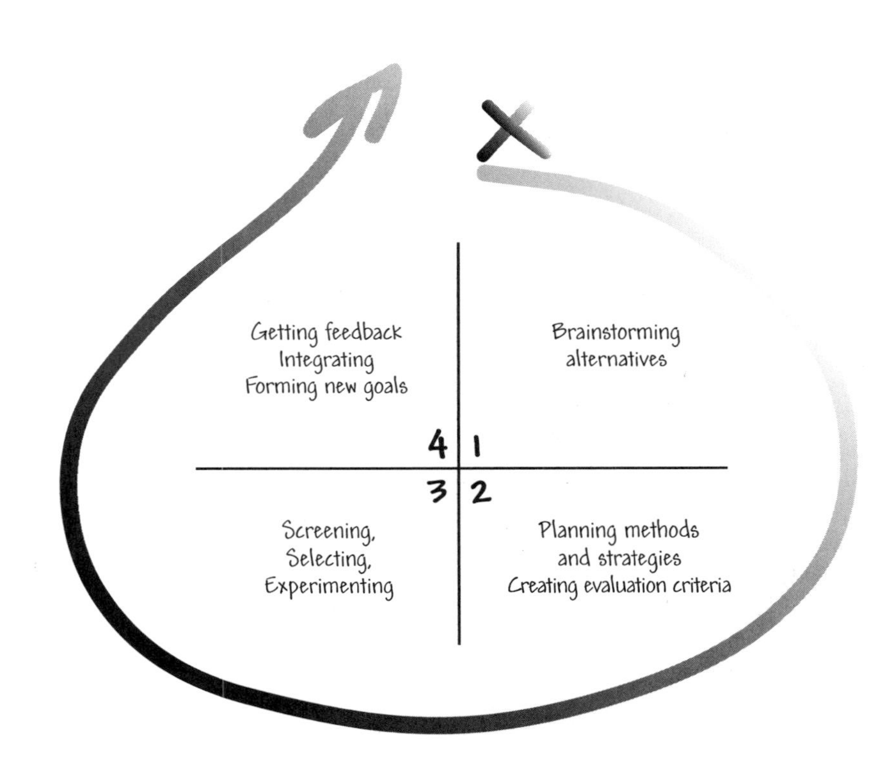

Proctor and Gamble Study, 1976

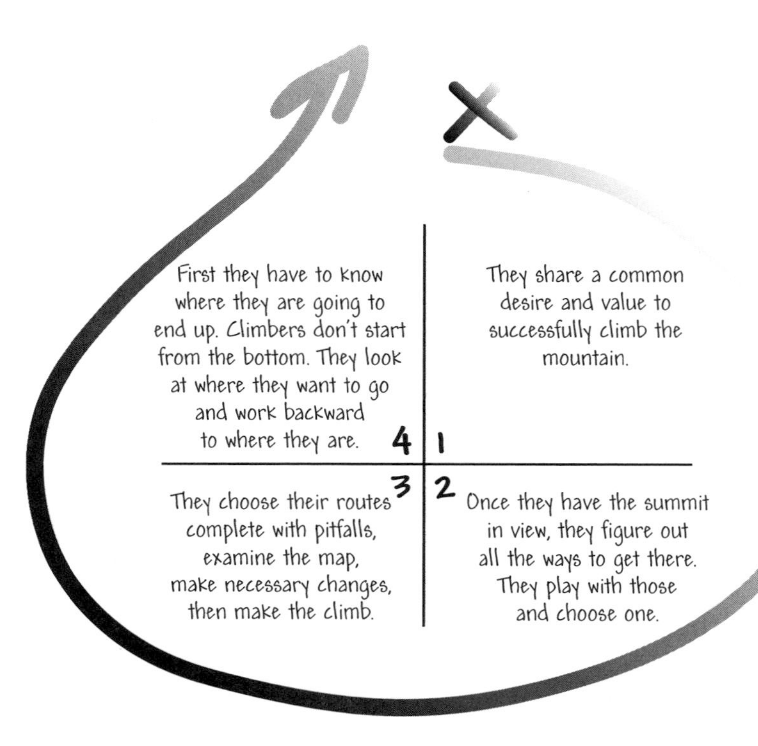

Warren Bennis using a mountain-climbing metaphor.

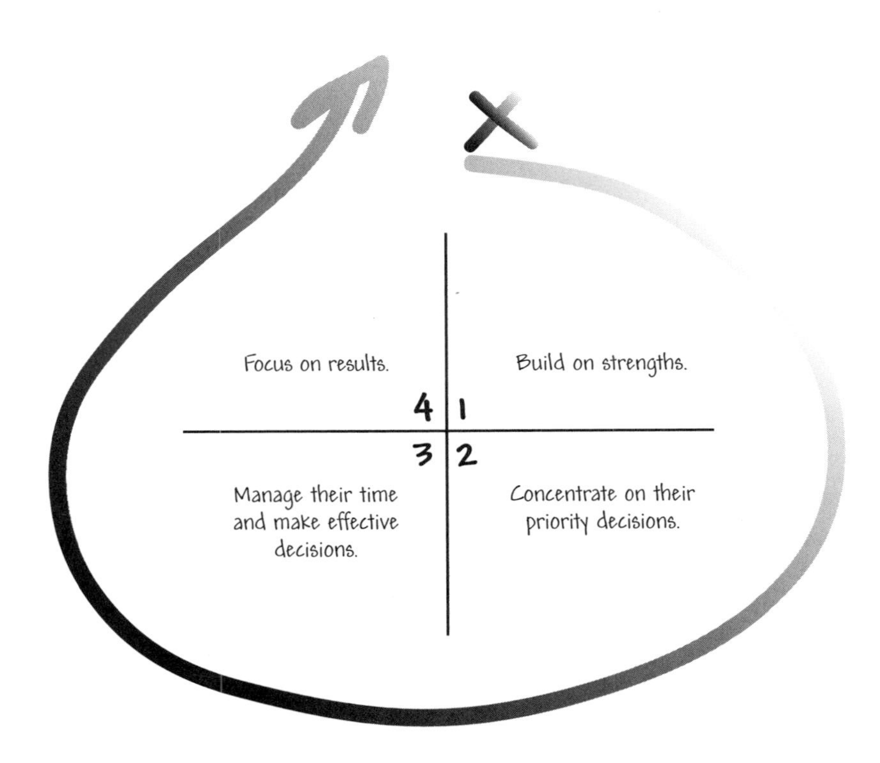

Peter Drucker

You must believe
in the intrinsic worth of people's diversity.

Help people reach their potential,
give the gift of space.

The way we touch each other is at the heart of who we are.
— Max DePree

Wholeness in organizations
comes from balance –
people and structures
aligned with vision and operations.

For this kind of balance
we need wisdom,
the wisdom of experience and thoughtfulness.

For this kind of balance
we need grace,
the grace of action reflected upon and acted anew.

We need to travel the cycle.

Organizations that travel the cycle are learning organizations.

EPILOGUE

Intelligence and the Cycle

A Learner's Story

When Leah was a freshman in high school, she enjoyed her new friends and she liked some of her teachers. But she had a fierce need to learn and school was not nearly exciting enough for her. There was so much deadening stuff, memorizing endless facts that were totally irrelevant to her life. She felt a real sadness because there was so much she desperately wanted to learn. She had a wonderful randomness that often took hold of her and, when that happened, her focus was so intense time became meaningless. Her teachers came to regard her randomness as a liability. They felt it took her away from "the things she needed to know."

When she asked her teachers why she had to memorize things that had no meaning in her life, they answered, "You'll need to know this later on," or "You want good grades to get into college, don't you?" or they simply frowned and ignored her questions.

At first she persevered, trying to add excitement to her studies by coming up with variations on assignments. In place of an essay, she offered to interview people and present her findings in a skit. Instead of a juvenile justice report to be encapsulated from her social studies text, she asked to be allowed to go to juvenile court and see for herself. Her teachers seldom agreed to her proposals and after a while she stopped trying. She had natural leadership talent and fulfilled this ability through her extracurricular activities, the one part of school she came to love. For her fierce need to learn she turned outside of school, where her randomness wasn't enough without the necessary structure a true education provides. She graduated, but the time spent was not happy or rewarding, and she has believed ever since that real learning does not happen in school. If you ask her today what she remembers most about high school, she will smile ruefully and repeat the question put to her most often, "Leah, why can't you be like everyone else?"

What is intelligence if not the ability
to face problems
in an unprogrammed (creative) manner?

The notion that such a nebulous,
socially defined concept
as intelligence
might be identified as a "thing"
with a locus in the brain
and a definite degree of heritability
– and that it might be measured as a single number
thus permitting a unilinear ranking of people
according to the amount they possess
is a principal error…
one that has reverberated throughout the country
and has affected millions of lives.
— Stephen Jay Gould

Intelligence is
a complex,
interdependent system
whereby we make meaning
through
experiencing life,
understanding knowledge,
solving problems and making decisions,
and creating and shaping environments
that sustain and renew our growth and well-being.

The entire process is one of meaning-making,
a process that leads us to understand how we are
both of life and in life.

Researchers and educators have long sought
to measure intelligence,
usually to rank people in terms of how much
or how little they have.

In light of the complexity of intelligence,
the results are ludicrous.
The paltry measures used are clearly
insufficient to even begin to measure
the capacity each of us has for knowing.

"Knowing" — think of all that means.

Knowing is:

Knowing what it is –
is to experience and internalize the knowledge.

Knowing that –
is about information.

Knowing how –
is body knowledge, being able to do.

Knowing your way around –
is functioning sucessfully in the cultural context of the situation.
— David Perkins

As long as the individual accepts and values himself,
he will continue to grow and develop his potentialities.
When he does not accept and value himself,
much of his energies will be used to
defend rather than to explore and to actualize himself.
— Clark Moustakas

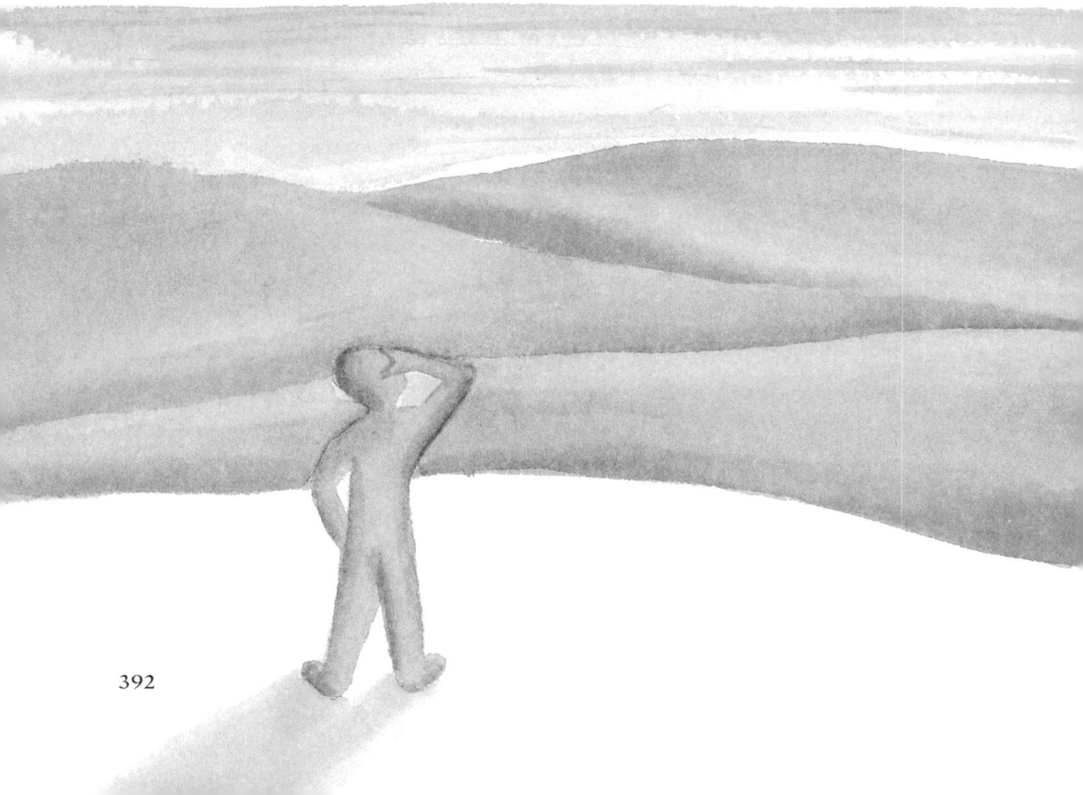

To judge my intelligence in **Quadrant One**,
you would have to know my life experiences,
the degree of diversity or blandness of my world.

You would have to know about the supports
I have in my life, the climate,
loving or threatening,
the trust I carry with me about people.

You would have to know
the safety of my world.
If I am not safe and I know it,
my focus is taken away from observing
as an intimate curiosity
and becomes a riveting attention to survival –
a very different enterprise.

We bring our own history when we make meaning,
and the person that I am today
sees my world from behind my eyes.
What I see and feel
is largely the result of where I have been.

You would have to know all that
to even begin to assess
my Quadrant One intelligence.

We cannot even begin to say
what an intelligence is
until we first ascertain
what kinds of knowledge
are available to it.
— Jeremy Campbell

To judge my intelligence in **Quadrant Two**,
you would have to know
how many opportunities I have had to know,
what kind of knowledge and what degree of excellence
have been made available to me
or withheld from me.

You would have to know my ability to conceptualize,
whether I can chunk knowledge into meaningful cores or structures
to get to the essence.
You would need to know how I connect
new conceptual systems to familiar ones.

You would have to know how skilled I am
at naming, at classifying, at sequencing,
at analyzing, at generalizing,
at metaphorizing.

You would have to know if the excellent ideas
my culture validates are congruent with my personal world.
If they are not, you would need to know
what meaning I am making of that.

You would have to know the level of formal education
I have been afforded and how well I succeeded in those places.
Were they narrow and rigid or expansive and open?

You would have to know whose voices have been excluded
from my knowing, what voices I have not heard
or not been allowed to hear, inadvertently or deliberately.

You would have to know all that to judge
my intelligence in Quadrant Two.

We do not realize
the sophistication
and highly developed
skills it takes
for any creature
to truly live in a wild system.
— David Whyte

To judge my intelligence in **Quadrant Three**,
you would have to know how practical my teachers were.
Did they teach me to use what I learned,
or was taking the test the only use I had to worry about?

You would have to know how well I manage my world,
from the trivial to the formidable.

You would have to know the record of my problem-solving
and decision-making,
how much I learn from my good tries, my "almosts,"
and my successes,
and whether or not I try again when I fail.

You would have to know whether
the environment in which I find myself
taps my potential. Or whether it drains it.

You would have to know something about
the resources that had been made available to me
to help me become.

You would have to know all this
to judge my intelligence in Quadrant Three.

To be
what we are capable of becoming
is the only end of life.
— Robert Louis Stevenson

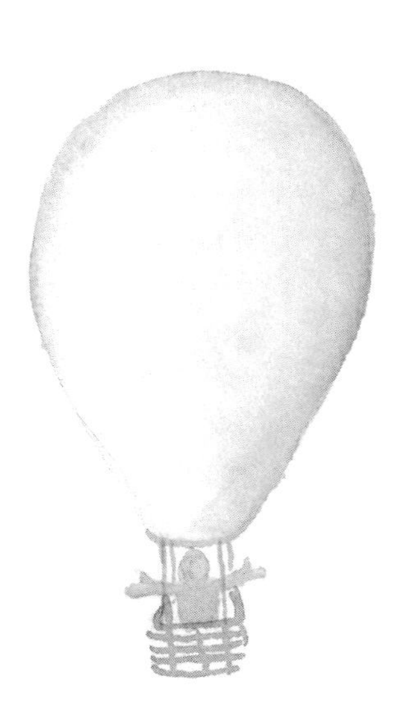

To judge my intelligence in **Quadrant Four**,
you would have to know how adaptive I am,
whether I shape my environment,
create new clearings.
You would need to know how I deal with novelty,
how I cope with strangeness,
how I tolerate ambiguity.

You would have to know how much I know
that I cannot tell,
the store of experience and intuitiveness
born of my past into my present
that does not lend itself to easy expression.

You would have to know of my courage
or lack of it in choosing continuing growth.

You would have to know of my ability
to assess and reassess limits that are placed on me.

You would have to know of the boundaries
that I need to break through and whether
I can distinguish the ones that bind me
from the ones I need to keep.
And you would need to know how I have come to know that.

You would have to know all this
to judge my intelligence in Quadrant Four.

An intelligence is
a biological and psychological potential;
that potential is capable
of being realized
to a greater or lesser extent
as a consequence of
the experimental,
cultural,
and motivational factors
that affect a person.
— Howard Gardner

Let us study and judge intelligence
(when we judge it at all)
in relation to real-world behavior.

Let us cease and desist from labeling intelligence
as an endowment
given to some and not to others,
and instead clearly recognize the developmental nature
of how we learn
to use our powers of
insight,
intuition,
thought,
wit,
common sense,
savvy,
creativity
and ultimately wisdom.

Let us recognize as Vygotsky did
the strong social nature of learning.
The structures that form and develop our intelligence
are created through interactions with others
in the social environment.
Higher levels of cognitive functioning are not hidden
in the child, awaiting release.
They **are formed** through social interaction.

Works of art are of infinite solitude,
and no means of approach is so useless as criticism.
Only love can touch and hold them and be fair to them.
— Rainer Maria Rilke

A child is a work of art.

So children who are not played with,
talked to, sung to, read to,
interacted with,
socialized,
simply do not have an equal opportunity
to become what they are capable of.

They are works of art
who have not been touched
or held by love,
so no judgment of their intelligence
can ever be fair to them.

Their unnurtured lives
are the greatest of tragedies.

The glowing core of passion at 4MAT's heart
burns with hope especially for these children,
that the care we take to accompany them to places
of feeling, reflecting, thinking, and doing,
of analyzing and synthesizing,
may open for them
a world of worth and wisdom.

For them we need to excel around the cycle.

APPENDIX A

Examples of 4MAT Instructional Design from Education

The following five instructional designs
were written by teachers from five different
education levels: primary school, middle school,
high school, community college, and law school.
They cover science, math, literature, technical writing,
and attorney-client confidentiality,
and provide examples of single wheels,
multiple, interlocking wheels,
and wheels that are part of yearlong 4MAT curriculum designs.

Animal Survival by David Hamaker
Grade Level: Primary
Subject: Science
Concept: Animal Habitats
Duration: Two to Three Weeks

Students will learn the characteristics of animal habitats.

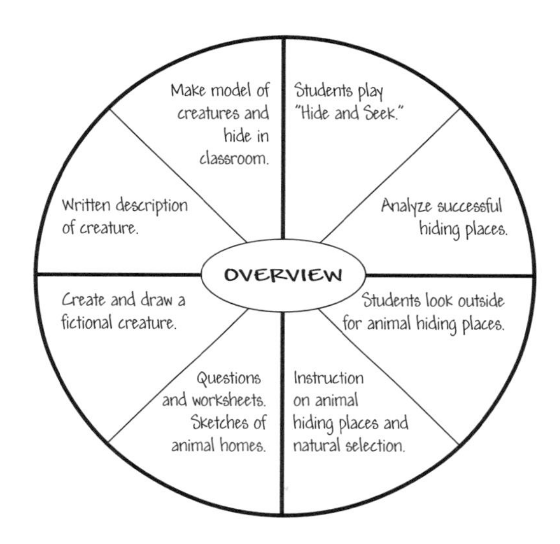

Quadrant One: Experiencing to Reflecting — Connections

R Mode: Connect
Students play Hide and Seek.

Objective: To create an experience that will lead students to an understanding of what they know instinctively about good and safe hiding places.

Activity: Students play Hide and Seek either indoors or outdoors. Students are selected to find hidden students.

Assessment: No student assessment for this step.
(Teacher self-assessment) Students' active involvement and enjoyment.

Quadrant One: Experiencing to Reflecting — Connections

L Mode: Examine
Students analyze successful hiding places.

Objective: To become more proficient at classifying positive and negative characteristics of hiding places.

Activity: Students work in small groups to answer the following:
Why were students found last more sucessful in hiding?
What makes a good hiding place?
What are the common features of good hiding places?
How are these features important to animals seeking shelter?

Assessment: (Students) Understanding of the concepts involved: students hand in their lists of the common features of good hiding places. Student contributions to their groups: students log the important contributions to their understanding from each member of their group.
(Teacher self-assessment) Quality of student engagement in the activity.

Quadrant Two: Reflecting to Conceptualizing — Concepts

R Mode: Image
Students look outside for animal hiding places.

Objective: To see the connection between what the students know and how animals instinctively apply the same criteria for survival.

Activity: After the teacher and students create the criteria list culled from the previous lesson step, students go outside and, working in small teams, use what they know about good hiding places to find spots which would be good hiding places for specific creatures, including insects, as well as animals such as squirrels, rabbits and other larger animals.

Assessment: (Students) Students' success at finding hiding places according to criteria set.
(Teacher self-assessment) Student skill at connection and focus outdoors.

Quadrant Two: Reflecting to Conceptualizing — Concepts

L Mode: Define
Teacher gives instruction on animal survival and animal hiding places.

Objective: To become more knowledgeable about how animal hiding places contribute to the process of animal survival.

Activity: Teacher provides information and illustrations on the necessary concepts, including vocabulary. Students read appropriate texts. Students watch appropriate videos and CDs.

Assessment: (Students) Understanding of the concepts involved: students take a facts test on the lecture and information.
(Teacher self-assessment) Quality of student understanding.

Quadrant Three: Conceptualizing to Doing — Applications

L Mode: Try
Students create sketches of animal homes and fill out prepared worksheets.

Objective: To provide guided practice on the concept of animal survival and new vocabulary.

Activity: Students answer questions from the text and videos and complete teacher-prepared worksheets. Students find animal hiding places in their own yards at home. Students make a list of what they find and sketch their findings. Opportunity will be given to share their findings.

Assessment: (Students) Understanding of the concepts involved: students hand in their sketches and their lists.
(Teacher self-assessment) Ascertain if any reteach is necessary.

Quadrant Three: Conceptualizing to Doing — Applications

R Mode: Extend
Students create a drawing of a fictional creature.

Objective: To extend what has been learned coupled with an imaginative creation of "animalness."

Activity: Students create a drawing of a fictional creature. The creature needs to be easily hidden in the classroom. Creature likeness should be lifesize.

Assessment: (Students) Completion of the project, congruence with rubric* created by teacher and students prior to the assignment.
(Teacher self-assessment) Quality of student imaginative risk-taking.

*A rubric is a written description of a scoring system that describes the necessary elements for grades A, B, C, etc.

Quadrant Four: Doing to Experiencing — Creation

L Mode: Refine
Students create a written description of their creature.

Objective: To expand the fictional creature project and use what they have learned about natural selection.

Activity: Students develop written descriptions of their creatures including: name, size, shape, color, special features. Students then work in groups of four to predict how successful each member's creature will be in hiding in the classroom.

Assessment: (Students) Quality of the written descriptions.
Assistance given to other group members.
(Teacher self-assessment) Student skill level in group contributions.

Quadrant Four: Doing to Experiencing — Creation

R Mode: Integrate
Students make their models and hide them in the classroom.

Objective: To complete a creative example of what was learned.

Activity: Students will create paper models of their creatures. Creatures are hidden in the classroom while members try to find them. Discuss success or lack of success in hiding the creatures, then try again. This time invite another class in to find them.

Assessment: (Students) Quality of completed projects based on an agreed-upon rubric.
(Teacher self-assessment) Quality of student engagement in the activity.

Resources: Illustrations for direct instruction, drawing materials, and sculpture materials.

David Hamaker teaches fourth grade at Riverview Elementary School, Marion Community School, Marion, Indiana. He has been a classroom teacher for seven years.

Symbols by Vera Hayes
Grade Level: Middle School
Subject: Mathematics
Concept: Symbols
Duration: Two weeks

A Three-Wheel Spiral — Wheel One of Three

Note that Wheels One and Two are only partial wheels. They go from Quadrant One, R Mode to Quadrant Three, L Mode. The performance assessment required in this unit, Quadrant Three, R Mode to Quadrant Four, L and R Mode does not happen until the third wheel.

Students will learn the concepts of symbols and how they apply not only in math, but in their everyday lives.

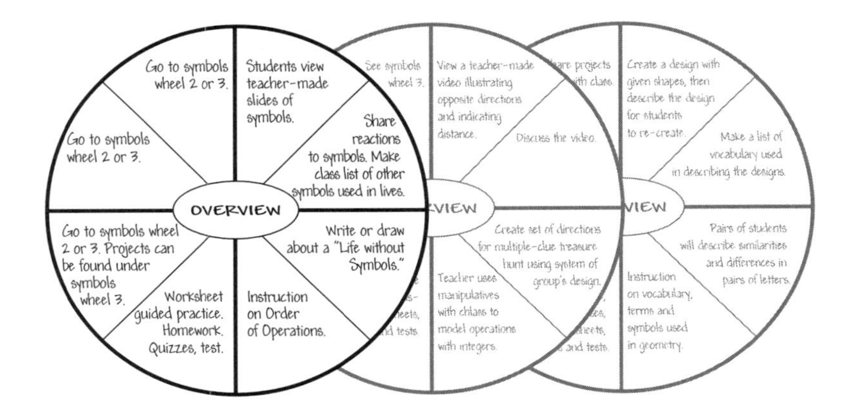

Quadrant One: Experiencing to Reflecting — Connections

R Mode: Connect
Students view teacher-made slides of symbols.

Objective: To create an awareness of the variety and number of symbols involved in our lives.

Activity: Students view teacher-made slides of symbols found in their environments, *e.g.*, McDonald's Arches, *etc*. Students write their initial reactions to the symbols as they are shown.

Assessment: No student assessment for this step.
(Teacher self-assessment) Students' active involvement and reactions.

Quadrant One: Experiencing to Reflecting — Connections

L Mode: Examine
Students share reactions to the symbols.
Students then make a class list of other symbols in their lives.

Objective: To analyze reactions to slides. Students need to come to understand that symbols often take the place of many words and may have different meanings to different people.

Activity: Students work in small groups sharing their reactions to each symbol. Discussion concerns the use of and our dependency on symbols. A class list of other symbols in our lives is created by the students with the teacher. Students are asked to comment on the purpose of symbols.

Assessment: (Students) Understanding of the concepts involved: students hand in their comments on the purpose of symbols in our lives. Student contributions to their groups: students log the most important contributions to their understanding from each member of their group.
(Teacher self-assessment) Quality of student engagement in the activity.

Quadrant Two: Reflecting to Conceptualizing — Concepts

R Mode: Image
Write or draw about a life without symbols.

Objective: To deepen the connection between symbols and our everyday lives.

Activity: In groups of four, students write or draw a situation illustrating life without symbols using rubric. Group creations are shared with the class.

Assessment: (Students) Students' success at illustrating life without

symbols according to the preapproved rubric. Group participation skills.
(Teacher assessment) Ability of the group to complete the assignment.

Quadrant Two: Reflecting to Conceptualizing — Concepts

L Mode: Define
Teacher gives instruction on the order of operations.

Objective: To introduce the order of operations and evaluating expressions.

Activity: Students interpret this sentence without punctuation: Paul said the teacher is very intelligent. Ask the students to determine who is intelligent. Relate the importance of punctuation to the importance of symbols of operation in mathematics and how the order affects the answer.

Assessment: (Students) Students' understanding of the concepts involved: students share their note-taking with each other and then take a quiz on the lecture.
(Teacher self-assessment) Quality of student understanding.

Quadrant Three: Conceptualizing to Doing — Applications

L Mode: Try
Students take part in guided practice through homework, teacher-prepared worksheets.

Objective: To provide guided practice on the skill of order of operations and evaluating expressions.

Activity: Students complete teacher-prepared worksheets and exercises.

Assessment: (Students) Understanding of the concepts involved: students hand in their worksheets and take a quiz.
(Teacher self-assessment) Ascertain any necessity for reteach.

Note that Wheels One and Two are only partial wheels. They go from Quadrant One, R Mode to Quadrant Three, L Mode. The performance assessment required in this unit, Quadrant Three, R Mode to Quadrant Four, L and R Mode, does not happen until the third wheel.

Continuation of Symbols by Vera Hayes
Grade Level: Middle School
Subject: Mathematics
Concept: Symbols Duration: Two weeks

A Three-Wheel Spiral — Wheel Two of Three

The learners will view integers as opposite directions. The learner will perform operations with integers and rational numbers.

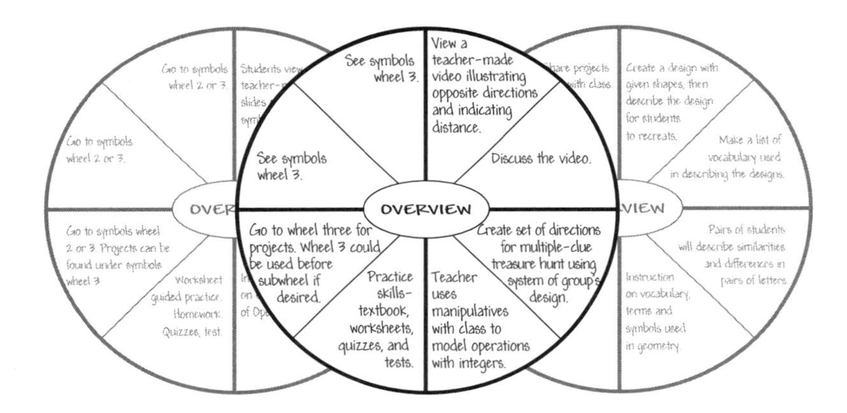

Quadrant One: Experiencing to Reflecting — Connections

R Mode: Connect
Students view teacher-made video illustrating opposite directions and indicating distance.

Objective: To create an image of distance, direction, and opposites.

Activity: Students view teacher-made video illustrating opposite directions and indicating distance: roller coaster, bouncing ball, escalators, elevators, see-saw, children swinging, road signs. Students write their initial reactions.

Assessment: No student assessment on this step.

(Teacher self-assessment) Students' active involvement and reactions.

Quadrant One: Experiencing to Reflecting — Connections

L Mode: Examine
Students discuss the video.

Objective: To analyze reactions to video. Students need to come to understand that every direction has an opposite and direction includes distance. Therefore, there is a need for integers/rational numbers and zero.

Activity: Students work in small groups sharing their reactions to the video. Students create a group list of their ideas.

Assessment: (Students) Understanding of the concepts involved: students hand in their comments with their group lists.
(Teacher self-assessment) Quality of student engagement in the activity.

Quadrant Two: Reflecting to Conceptualizing — Concepts

R Mode: Image
Create a set of directions for multiple-clue treasure hunt using system of group's design.

Objective: To deepen the connection between integers and their relationship to distance, direction, and opposites.

Activity: In groups of four, students create a set of directions for a multiple-clue treasure hunt using signs and numbers (no words or letters). Groups are allowed to leave the room to create an accurate set of directions to find the treasure on the school campus. Groups will exchange and follow clues to test their validity.

Assessment: (Students) Quality of teamwork and accuracy of understanding.
(Teacher self-assessment) Ability of the teams to function in the freedom of the campus and to complete the project well.

Quadrant Two: Reflecting to Conceptualizing — Concepts

L Mode: Define
Teacher models operations with integers using manipulatives.

Objective: To provide instruction on operations and properties with integers.

Activity: Teacher uses positive/negative chips as manipulatives. Teacher models opposites, absolute value, adding like/unlike signs, subtracting, multiplying, and dividing. Students "discover" rules.

Assessment: (Students) Understanding of the concepts involved: students share their note-taking examples, participation with manipulatives.
(Teacher self-assessment) Quality of student understanding.

Quadrant Three: Conceptualizing to Doing — Applications

L Mode: Try
Students take part in guided practice through textbook, homework, and a quiz.

Objective: To provide guided practice with integers and rational numbers.

Activity: Students complete text worksheets and a quiz.

Assessment: (Students) Understanding of the concepts involved: students hand in their worksheets and take a quiz.
(Teacher self-assessment) Ascertain any necessity for reteach.

Note that Wheels One and Two are only partial wheels.
They go from Quadrant One, R Mode to Quadrant Three, L Mode.
The performance assessment required in this unit, Quadrant Three, R Mode to Quadrant Four, L and R Mode, does not happen until the third wheel.

Continuation of Symbols by Vera Hayes
Grade Level: Middle School
Subject: Mathematics
Concept: Geometry Symbols

Duration: Ten days

A Three-Wheel Spiral — Wheel Three of Three

The learners will identify and use geometry symbols and vocabulary.

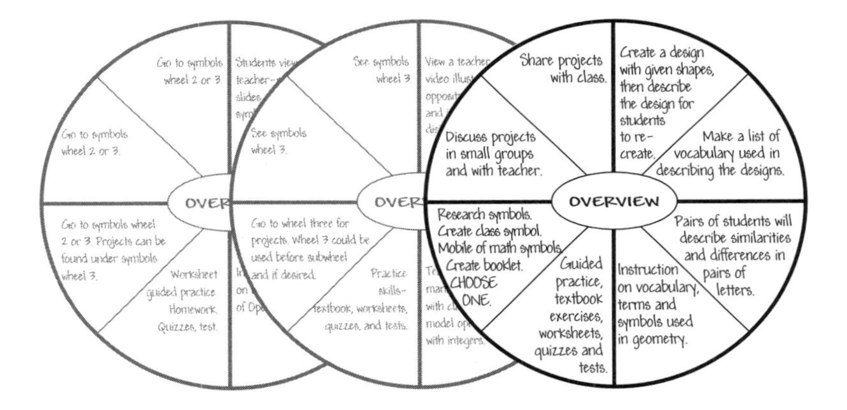

Quadrant One: Experiencing to Reflecting — Connections

R Mode: Connect
Students create a design with given shapes, then describe the design for fellow students to recreate.

Objective: To create an awareness of the need for correct vocabulary in geometry.

Activity: Students work in pairs. Each pair is given a set of geometric shapes to create a design. One student creates the design behind a barrier so her/his partner cannot see the design. The partner's description must be precise enough so that the exact same design can be built.

The partner creating the design may ask questions as directions are given. The partners then change roles and try again.

Assessment: No student assessment for this step.
(Teacher self-assessment) Participation in activity, attentiveness to partner.

Quadrant One: Experiencing to Reflecting — Connections

L Mode: Examine
Students make a list of vocabulary used in describing the designs.

Objective: To analyze experience and to enhance correct vocabulary in geometry.

Activity: Students make a list of the vocabulary used in describing their designs. The lists are then combined into a class list and posted. A discussion of the importance of correct vocabulary.

Assessment: (Students) Understanding of the concepts involved, number of words on the list, quality of the list.
(Teacher self-assessment) Quality of student engagement in the activity.

Quadrant Two: Reflecting to Conceptualizing — Concepts

R Mode: Image
Pairs of students will describe similarities and differences in pairs of letters.

Objective: To become aware that geometry vocabulary is also used to describe things other than geometric designs.

Activity: Pairs of students will choose any two letters from the alphabet and describe their similarities and differences. Each pair will exchange their descriptions with another pair of students and they then try to determine which letters are being described.

Assessment: (Students) Quality of work with partner, completeness of descriptions. Discussion of these requirements needs to take place beforehand.
(Teacher self-assessment) Student ability to complete the assignment.

QUADRANT TWO: REFLECTING TO CONCEPTUALIZING — CONCEPTS

L Mode: Define
Teacher gives instruction on terms, symbols, and vocabulary used in geometry.

Objective: To become more knowledgeable about geometry terms, symbols, and vocabulary.

Activity: Teacher provides information and illustrations on the terms and symbols and vocabulary. Students read appropriate texts.

Assessment: (Students) Understanding of the concepts involved: students take a facts test on the lecture and information.
(Teacher self-assessment) Quality of student understanding.

QUADRANT THREE: CONCEPTUALIZING TO DOING — APPLICATIONS

L Mode: Try
Students engage in guided practice.

Objective: To provide guided practice with worksheets, textbook exercises, and quizzes.

Activity: Students answer questions from the text and complete worksheets. Students take a quiz.

Assessment: (Students) Understanding of the concepts involved: students hand in their worksheets and their quiz.
(Teacher self-assessment) Ascertain any necessity for reteach.

QUADRANT THREE: CONCEPTUALIZING TO DOING — APPLICATIONS

R Mode: Extend
Students research symbols and create a class symbol, or make a mobile of math symbols, or create a booklet.

Objective: To extend what has been learned by providing activities that will broaden students' experiences in the use of symbols.

Activity: Students select one of the following projects. They are given a timeline for check/edit day and project-due day. A rubric is supplied to them outlining grading procedures and project requirements.

1. Research the history of symbols in a specific area of use. Prepare a report either in poster or written form. Examples: history of the number system, geometric symbols, braille, the periodic table, traffic symbols.
2. Create a symbol that represents your math class. Display on a poster and write an explanation for the symbol.
3. Find as many mathematical symbols as possible. Organize them into "families" and display in a mobile.
4. Create a booklet about symbols and the order of operations or integers as if it were a teaching tool for a younger student. You should spice up your work to make the booklet interesting.
5. Create a set of cartoons illustrating the order of operations, integers, mathematical symbols or geometry vocabulary. (Some examples can be found in the book *Humor in Math.*)
6. Pretend you are an integer or a mathematical symbol. Write a story about your life.
7. Make a collage illustrating some idea about integers (opposite directions, ups-downs, opposite property, their uses.) Choose one to illustrate.

Assessment: (Students) This is a major performance assessment. Completion of the project, congruence with rubric created by teacher and students prior to the assignment.
(Teacher assessment) Quality of student imaginative risk-taking.

Quadrant Four: Doing to Experiencing — Creation

L Mode: Refine
Students discuss their projects in small groups and with their teacher.

Objective: To give guidance and feedback to students' plans, to encourage, to refine.

Activity: Students discuss projects in small groups and with their teacher.

Assessment: (Students) Quality of the plans, timelines, participation. Assistance given to other group members.
(Teacher self-assessment) Student skill level in group contributions.

Quadrant Four: Doing to Experiencing — Creation

R Mode: Integrate
Students do their projects and share them with the class.

Objective: To complete a creative example and to delight in what was learned.

Activity: Students will create their projects and share them with the class.

Assessment: (Students) Quality of completed projects based on an agreed upon rubric.
(Teacher self-assessment) Quality of student engagement in the activity.

Resources: Math textbook with unit on Order of Operations.
Humor in Math, National Council of Teachers of Mathematics.
Slides of sheet music, symbols of local business logos, college symbols, school symbols, Olympic symbol, medical symbols, religious symbols, symbols for editing, punctuation marks, clothes labels.

Vera Hayes teaches math at Eisenhower Middle School in North East Independent School District in San Antonio, Texas.

Personal and Collective Perspectives:
Thornton Wilder's *Our Town* by Lori Barnett
Grade Level: High School
Subject: Literature
Concept: Perspective — Individual and Universal
Duration: Two weeks

As part of an ongoing study of the concept of "Perspective" in junior English, students will examine the contrast between the individual and the universal as depicted in *Our Town* by Thorton Wilder and as reflected in the students' individual lives and the culture of their time.

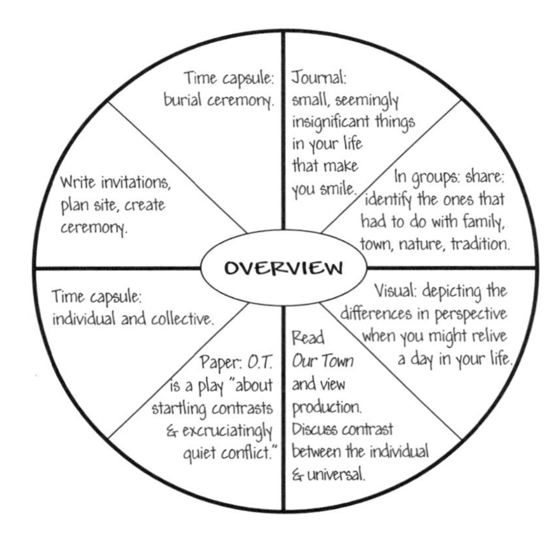

In 1991, as part of her early 4MAT training, Lori designed a three-wheel lesson on *Macbeth*. Her initial conceptual framework evolved from the issue of "Choices" to the wider one of "Perspectives." Gradually she realized that "Perspectives" could be the thread weaving the entire 11th grade literature program together, a curriculum she has now expanded to at least eight other 4MAT wheels including such works as Poe's short stories, *Huckleberry Finn, Tell Me Why the Caged Bird Sings, Catcher in the Rye, Ordinary People, Rich in Love, Walden,* and a unit on poetry. So successful was this curriculum design, over the next years she organized the 9th grade around the concept of "Independence and Interdependence," the 12th grade around the concept of "Passion" and envisions completing this high school curriculum with a possible "Journey" concept in the 10th grade. Many of her other wheels are available in *4MAT in Action K–6, 4MAT in Action 7–12,* and Excel's software 4MATION in the High School LESSON BANK.

Quadrant One: Experiencing to Reflecting — Connections

R Mode: Connect
Students create a journal of small, seemingly insignificant things in their lives that make them smile.

Objective: To create an awareness of the simple things in their lives that reverberate with meaning for them, thus establishing their personal, daily perspective.

Activity: In journals, students will make a comprehensive list of the small, seemingly insignificant things in their lives that make them smile. Students will share lists in group, noting patterns.

Assessment: (Students) Completion of journal entry. Quality of sharing.
(Teacher self-assessment) Non-trivial attention to the task.

Quadrant One: Experiencing to Reflecting — Connections

L Mode: Examine
In groups, students identify and classify the recorded items.

Objective: Students will begin to understand that their personal perspective is part of a larger socio/cultural perspective.

Activity: Student lists are classified under the four headings: house, family, town and nature. Classifications are reported in the large group.

Assessment: (Students) Understanding of the concepts involved, quality of the list, and completion of the task.
(Teacher self-assessment) Quality of student engagement in the activity.

Quadrant Two: Reflecting to Conceptualizing — Concepts

R Mode: Image
Students will visually illustrate differences in perspective.

Objective: To become aware of the differences in perspective one might have if one were to relive a day in one's life.

Activity: Using guided imagery from their teacher's life as an example, students choose a day in their lives to relive and create a representational or non-representational visual showing the difference in perspective between the two states of knowing: the first time and then the relived time.

Assessment: (Students) Strength of the visual, rubric given out prior to the assignment, and the ability to articulate the difference between the two states of knowing.
(Teacher self-assessment) Ability of the group to complete the assignment.

Quadrant Two: Reflecting to Conceptualizing — Concepts

L Mode: Define
Students read the play and view the theater presentation. Students discuss the contrast between the individual and the universal perspectives.

Objective: To explore the role of the stage manager as a character representing multiple states of knowing, thus multiple perspectives, and to examine different reviews of the play.

Activity: Students read the play and watch in-class presentations of key scenes. Students will discuss the role of the stage manager and analyze various reviews: a tribute to small-town life, a dark depiction of humanness, etc. Also the contrast between the individual and the universal depicted through language, character, set design and overall structure. Also the difference in the perspectives of the living and dead.

Assessment: (Students) Understanding of the concepts involved. Quality of drama presentations, quality of writing and discussion. All three rubrics presented beforehand.
(Teacher self-assessment) Quality of student understanding.

Quadrant Three: Conceptualizing to Doing — Applications

L Mode: Try
Students write an essay on perspective, as seen in contrasts and conflict.

Objective: To provide practice in analyzing a work of literature.

Activity: Students will compile lists of contrasts in perspective and their ensuing conflicts in the play, analyze the contrast between the individual and the universal in the stage manager's speeches, and write a major paper on the statement: "*Our Town* is a play about startling contrasts and excruciatingly quiet conflict."

Assessment: (Students) Caliber of the writing through student and teacher preapproved rubric.
(Teacher self-assessment) Ascertain any necessity for reteach.

Quadrant Three: Conceptualizing to Doing — Applications

R Mode: Extend
Students create time capsules.

Objective: To provide an opportunity for students to celebrate the individual and the collective, the present and the future perspectives of their own lives.

Activity: After rereading the speech in which the stage manager describes the time capsule Grovers Corners buried in the cornerstone of the bank, students will:

1. create individual mini-capsules they are to hide for a period of time.
2. create a large time capsule which typifies the life of a Ridgewood High School student living in the present in New Jersey. Music, literature, art, photographs, objects, etc. are to be included.

Assessment: (Students) This is a major performance assessment. Completion of the project, congruence with rubric created by teacher and students prior to the assignment.
(Teacher assessment) Quality of student imagination and originality.

Quadrant Four: Doing to Experiencing — Creation

L Mode: Refine
Students prepare to conduct their capsule burial ceremony.

Objective: To give practice in evaluating the capsule as a true representation of themselves and their culture.

Activity: Students in committees evaluate the selections for the large time capsule and then create a time capsule ceremony with appropriate content, invitations to the present ceremony and the future one, choosing appropriate burial site with official approval, speeches and music, publicity and yearbook notification.

Assessment: (Students) Quality of the plans, timelines, participation. Assistance given to other group members.
(Teacher self-assessment) Student skill level in group contributions.

Quadrant Four: Doing to Experiencing — Creation

R Mode: Integrate
Students conduct the burial ceremony.

Objective: To celebrate the individual as well as the collective; the small and the large; the present and the future perspectives.

Activity: Students will conduct the burial ceremony and invite guests to the unearthing in 25 years.

Assessment: (Students) Quality and smoothness of the ceremony based on an agreed-upon rubric.

(Teacher assessment) Quality of student engagement in the activity.

Resources: *New York Times* theater reviews from prominent productions. Copies of *Our Town,* video of Hal Holbrook version, time capsule objects, school burial site.

Lori Barnett is an English teacher and Staff Development Leader in the Ridgewood, NJ schools. She is a certified 4MAT trainer and consultant.

Precision and Form in Written Language by Mary Bess Dunn
Grade Level: Community College
Subject: English
Concept: Precision and Form in Written Language
Duration: One week

Students will learn the components of effective, organized written communication.

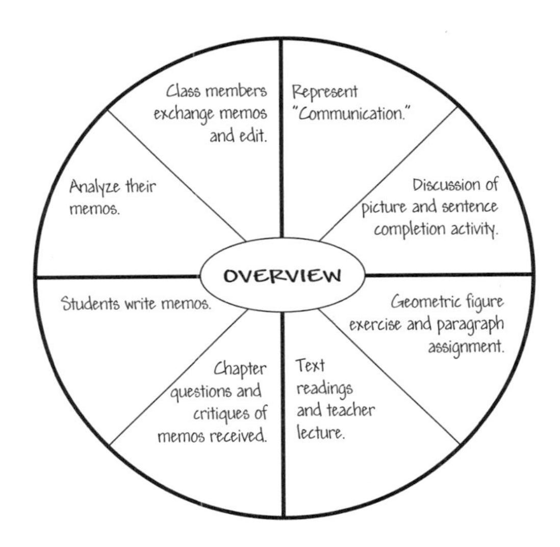

QUADRANT ONE: EXPERIENCING TO REFLECTING — CONNECTIONS

R Mode: Connect
Students create a representation of the communication concept.

Objective: To create an awareness for students demonstrating how communication impacts them in their everyday lives.

Activity: Divide the class into groups of five. The groups are told to discuss the concept of communication. Using blank newsprint and markers provided, draw a representation of communication. The students may approach this task in any way that is comfortable for them.

All group members sign the image and tape it up on the wall in the classroom.

Assessment: (Students) Completion of representation. Quality of sharing.
(Teacher self-assessment) Non-trivial attention to the task.

Teacher's Note: I have used this activity with numerous groups and have never had the same picture repeated. This activity works very well as a Quadrant One, Right Mode experience.

Quadrant One: Experiencing to Reflecting — Connections

L Mode: Examine
Students combine their findings and interpretations.

Objective: Students will develop a composite description of what the class thinks communication means in the broadest sense.

Activity: The large group takes each picture and requests interpretations from each group. Reactions and comments are given. Then the students are asked to complete the following stem: This activity...

Assessment: (Students) Understanding of the concepts involved, quality of the descriptions and attention to fellow students.
(Teacher self-assessment) Quality of student engagement in the activity.

Teacher's Note: I always display a composite of the sentence stem completions at the beginning of the next class session.

Quadrant Two: Reflecting to Conceptualizing — Concepts

R Mode: Image
Students will experience the need for precision in writing.

Objective: For the students to integrate the experience in Quadrant One with a need to expand their present writing skill levels.

Activity: Using a pair of volunteers, give one a drawing of an intricate geometric figure. The first volunteer is to tell the other volunteer how to draw the figure on the chalkboard. The person drawing and the person describing must stand so they cannot see each other.

The drawer may not speak to the describer, the receiver is at the mercy of the sender, exactly as happens in written communication.

Ask for a second pair of volunteers. They have the same task with another drawing except that they may both speak but not look at each other. The drawer may ask for clarification. This approximates telephone communication.

A third pair of volunteers has another task with a new drawing; the describer may watch the drawer and they may communicate freely, approximating face-to-face communication.

Students then write a paragraph relating this activity to their own experiences with these different kinds of communication as well as their own skill development needs.

Assessment: (Students) Precision of word choice and honesty. Rubric given out prior to the assignment.

(Teacher self-assessment) Did the assignment encompass the major communication issues?

Quadrant Two: Reflecting to Conceptualizing — Concepts

L Mode: Define
Students will hear expert knowledge.

Objective: To teach the form, style and organization of a memorandum.

Activity: Students will read assigned text chapter. Teacher will lecture using text as a base.

Assessment: (Students) Understanding of the concepts involved, test given on concepts from the lecture and the text.
(Teacher self-assessment) Quality of student understanding.

Quadrant Three: Conceptualizing to Doing — Applications

L Mode: Try
Students study chapter questions and write critiques of memos.

Objective: To provide guided practice in writing memos.

Activity: Students will do activities at the end of text chapter. Students will bring memos received or written to class. Students will critique their memos and rewrite them.
Assessment: (Students) Quality of memos and critiques.
(Teacher self-assessment) Ascertain any necessity for reteach.

Quadrant Three: Conceptualizing to Doing — Applications

R Mode: Extend
Students write memos.

Objective: To use their skill.

Activity: Students will each write a first draft of a memo to a member of the next technical writing class informing them as to date and time of class meetings, location of class, personal perceptions of course content, and effectiveness of instruction. (They are free to be honest.)

Assessment: (Students) Evaluation of their first drafts.
(Teacher self-assessment) Quality of student skill.

Quadrant Four: Doing to Experiencing — Creation

L Mode: Refine
Students will edit and refine their first drafts.

Objective: To polish a work in progress.

Activity: Students complete their memos.

Assessment: (Students) Quality of the finished memo. Rubric approved prior to the assignment.
(Teacher self-assessment) Determine any remediation needs.

Quadrant Four: Doing to Experiencing — Creation

R Mode: Integrate
To assist each other in refining their skills.

Objective: To teach each other and to evaluate the learning.

Activity: Class partners exchange memos and critique for each other.

Assessment: (Students) Quality of the finished product.
(Teacher self-assessment) How well did the unit work?

Resources: Newsprint and markers, geometric figures.

Mary Bess Dunn was at the time of this writing Asstistant Professor of Reading and Special Education at Tennessee State University, Nashville, TN.

Attorney/Client Confidentiality by Cindy Kelly Conlon

Grade Level: Law School
Subject: Graduate Law – Social Studies
Concept: Attorney/Client Confidentiality
Duration: Two weeks

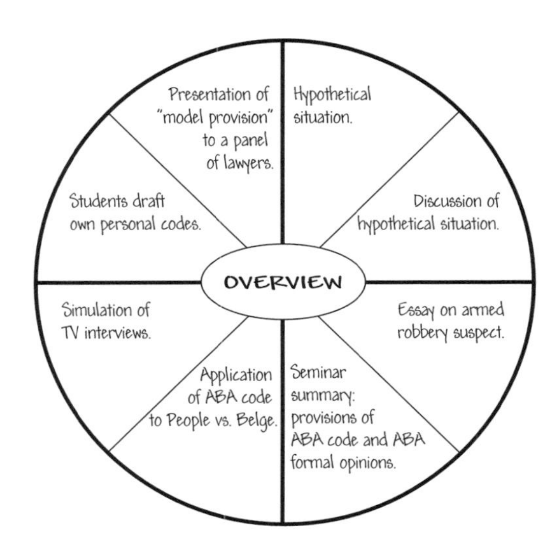

Quadrant One: Experiencing to Reflecting — Connections

R Mode: Connect
To simulate a hypothetical situation.

Objective: To introduce the concept of confidentiality. To allow students to clarify their own values concerning confidentiality.

Activity: Present students with the following hypothetical:

You and your best law school friend are talking, and your friend informs you that she has applied for a position on the law review staff. Because her grades were not high enough to qualify, she has submitted an antitrust article in response to a complicated problem which the law review staff assigned. You ask to look at the article and are amazed. The writing style is clear and crisp, the content is well organized, and the proposed solution is brilliant. In fact, you are so impressed that, while you know your friend is a good student and a fairly talented writer, you realize she could not possibly have written this article by herself. When you press her, she admits that a lawyer from a prominent antitrust firm actually wrote the draft, and she merely rewrote this draft. She begs you not to tell anyone. This is her only chance to make the law review and hopefully get a job with a prestigious law firm.

Ask the students whether or not they would tell anyone at the law school about the woman's action. Pose the following questions:

Do they have a duty to tell anyone?
Do they have a duty not to tell anyone?
From what sources do such duties arise?
Would their feelings be different if any of the following were true?
a. You are one of the editors of the law review staff.
b. You are currently a member of the law review staff.
c. You are a student also competing for a position on the law review staff.

Assessment: (Students) Level of conceptual understanding as to the nature of the dilemma. Quality of discussion participation.
(Teacher self-assessment) Success of the simulation in raising key concepts.

Quadrant One: Experiencing to Reflecting — Connections

L Mode: Examine
Discussion of hypothetical.

Objective: To help students identify the values of loyalty and privacy underlying the concept of confidentiality and the competing societal need for accurate information.

Activity: A discussion of the students' responses to the hypothetical.
Did their feelings change in response to any of the situations presented?
If so, what additional factors were relevant?
What underlying values ultimately shaped their responses?
Through what process did they decide?
How did they balance their loyalty to a friend against their responsibility as a member of the law school community?
How was their own self-interest affected?

Assessment: (Students) Quality of analysis and participation.
(Teacher self-assessment) Quality of student engagement in the activity.

Quadrant Two: Reflecting to Conceptualizing — Concepts

R Mode: Image
Essay on armed robbery suspect.

Objective: To introduce the concept of confidentiality in the context of the attorney/client relationship. To allow students to identify their own values about how this concept applies in the context of criminal defense.

Activity: Ask each student to write a short in-class response to the following problem:

You are a public defender who has been assigned to represent a man who has been charged with armed robbery. In your first interview, the client tells you that he has committed a series of burglaries in the same neighborhood. In fact, he burglarized a house (taking money and some jewelry) only a few hours before he robbed the gas station which is the basis of this charge. He has not been charged with any of the other burglaries. As far as he knows, he is not even a suspect.

What is your ethical obligation to your client regarding his admissions?
Can you defend him on the armed robbery charge knowing that he committed the crime?
Do you have any obligation to inform anyone of the fact that he has also committed other burglaries?

After each student has responded individually in writing, class discussion should follow posing the following questions:

Does the attorney have any obligation to keep his client's admissions a secret?
Is his duty the same regarding information concerning both the robbery and the burglaries?
What if the burglaries occurred in the attorney's own neighborhood?
What values support the view that the attorney should maintain all of a client's confidences?
Are those values any different from the values identified in the situation discussed in Quadrant One of this unit? (Loyalty owed to a friend, *etc.*)
What values support the view that the attorney should inform the police about a client's involvement in the burglaries?
How would you balance these competing values?

Assessment: (Students) The quality of the students' essays in terms of their deepening understanding of the essence of the confidentiality concept.
(Teacher self-assessment) Is there sufficient grounding in the concept?

Quadrant Two: Reflecting to Conceptualizing — Concepts

L Mode: Define
Summary: Provisions of the ABA code and ABA formal opinions.

Objective: To identify the provisions of the American Bar Association Code of Professional Responsibility that define the attorney's ethical responsibilities in this situation.

Activity: Students read assigned materials which outline ethical duties in terms of client confidences:
Canon four of the ABA Code
ABA Formal Opinion 287 (1953)
Formal Opinion 341 (1930)
Formal Opinion 23 (1930)
Formal Opinion 87 (1932)
Formal Opinion 155 (1936)
Formal Opinion 156 (1936)

Teacher summarizes the readings, using a seminar format.

Assessment: (Students) Understanding of the concepts involved. Quality of student participation.
(Teacher self-assessment) Quality of student understanding.

QUADRANT THREE: CONCEPTUALIZING TO DOING — APPLICATIONS

L Mode: Try
Application of ABA code.

Objective: To apply the principles of the ABA Code to a particular factual situation: the *People* vs. *Belge*.

Activity: Students read the article "Problem 9, the Requirement of Candor" from Part II, *The Garrow Case* and decide whether or not the attorneys in the case followed their ethical obligations under the ABA Code of Professional Responsibility.

After discussing their own decisions regarding the attorneys' behavior, inform the students about the decision of the group that had the responsibility for imposing discipline on the attorneys in this case. (The New York State Bar Committee on Professional Ethics, Opinion No. 479, March 6, 1978 holding that: "The lawyer was under an injunction not to disclose to the Authorities his knowledge of the two prior murders, and was duty-bound not to reveal to the Authorities the location of the bodies.")

Ask the students whether they agree or disagree with this decision. What purpose would have been served by imposing some sanction on the attorneys in this case? If a sanction had been imposed, what type of sanction would have been appropriate: censure, suspension from practice, disbarment?

Regardless of whether disciplinary sanctions were imposed on the attorneys for violating their ethical duties, should the attorneys have been indicted for violating any criminal laws? In the actual case, one attorney was indicted for violating statutes which require that a decent burial be accorded the dead and that anyone knowing of the death of a person without medical assistance report that knowledge to Authorities. *People* vs. *Belge*, 83 Misc. 2d 186, 373 N.Y.S. 2d 798, 1975.

Assessment: (Students) Quality of understanding of the concepts and participation.
(Teacher self-assessment) Ascertain any reteach needs.

Quadrant Three: Conceptualizing to Doing — Applications

R Mode: Extend
Simulation of TV interviews.

Objective: To examine the ethical issues in this case from the perspective of the entire community. To explore students' feelings about the ethical issues presented. To identify the process by which students would resolve a conflict between their own moral values and their ethical duties as attorneys.

Activity: Students participate in a simulation of a television interview examining the attorneys' actions in the case they read above, in Quadrant Three, Left Mode.

Each member of the panel presents his/her own view of the propriety of the attorneys' actions in this case. Members of the audience then ask questions of the panel. The panel consists of the following individuals:

The attorneys in this case
The father of one of the victims
The Chief of Police
A member of the New York State Bar Committee on Professional Ethics

Students in the class should assume their own roles which reflect a diverse group of the community. The teacher serves as moderator, pressing each panelist to either defend or criticize the attorneys' actions.

Following the simulations, students should share their reactions.

Was the simulation realistic?
How did the students feel assuming the roles of nonlawyers?
Did they feel that the community members had valid criticisms of the lawyers' behavior?
What values were represented by the participants' comments?
Should those values be recognized in the Code of Professional Responsibility?
If so, how? If not, why not?

Assessment: (Students) Realism of panel and quality of conceptual understanding.
(Teacher self-assessment) Quality of student imagination and originality.

QUADRANT FOUR: DOING TO EXPERIENCING — CREATION

L Mode: Refine
Students draft their own personal codes.

Objective: To get a clear picture of the students' understanding of the values underlying the concept of confidentiality.

Activity: Each students drafts a provision of a model code of professional responsibility, defining the nature of the attorney's duty to preserve a client's confidences. The code should include both a statement of the ethical standard, as well as background "comments" which explain the values underlying the code.

Assessment: (Students) Thoroughness and range of issues identified in students' codes.
(Teacher self-assessment) Ability of the students to explore the complexity of this issue.

QUADRANT FOUR: DOING TO EXPERIENCING — CREATION

R Mode: Integrate
Presentation of "model provision" to a panel of nonlawyers.

Objective: To give students the opportunity to share their insights about the strengths and weaknesses of the current code provisions regarding confidentiality. To explain their views to a group of nonlawyers. To identify and defend the values underlying their views.

Activity: Students share their model code provisions and are asked to vote for one such provision which reflects the consensus of the group by at least a simple majority. The students will present this model provision to a panel of nonlawyers.
The panel should consist of:
A faculty member from the philosophy department
A physician
A priest, minister or rabbi
A business executive
A high school principal

The panel members should evaluate the proposed code provision in terms of their view of the purpose of attorney/client confidentiality in our society. Students should respond to any questions or criticisms raised by panel members. At the end of the discussion, each student should write a short statement as an addendum to his or her own model code provision which describes reactions to the discussion. Would the student now revise his or her draft provision in any way? Why or why not?

Assessment: (Students) Quality of students' understanding of the legal issues and underlying values in both written and panel participation.
(Teacher self-assessment) Quality of student engagement in the activity.

Resources: Teacher-prepared scenario case study; panel of guests.
Annotated Code of Professional Responsibility, American Bar Association, Chicago, IL, 1979.
Opinions of the Committee on Professional Ethics, American Bar Association, Chicago, IL, 1967.
Redlich, Norman, *Professional Responsibility: A Problem Approach.* Boston, MA: Little, Brown and Co., 1976, pp. 60-62.

Cindy Kelly Conlon J.D., Ph. D. was at the time of this writing an Assistant Professor of Law at Loyola University School of Law in Chicago, Illinois. She is a certified 4MAT trainer and consultant.

Appendix B

Examples of 4MAT Instructional Design from Management

The following two Instructional Designs come from Linda Lindsey, Director, Excel Management Division

City Managers and Recycling

Several years ago I worked with department heads in a medium-sized southern city. I asked each manager to bring in notes on a problem her/his department had tried to solve during the past year, successfully or unsucessfully.

Each manager created a narrative list of the steps followed in the attempt to solve the problem. We cut out the individual steps and taped them onto a 4MAT wheel on a large paper chart. In every case of problem-solving that had come to unsuccessful conclusion, all the steps taken fell within Quadrants Two and Three, and no steps had been taken in Quadrants One and Four.

In every case, the problems that had been solved successfully used strategies taken from all four quadrants.

In the case of the recycling initiative, there had been successes, but also major problems:

The city only purchased one kind of recycling container.

Families were assigned only one container.

The initial letter to the citizens did not clearly specify what items could and could not be recycled.

Several thousand empty containers were stolen from curbs.

When staff analyzed the recycling initiative in light of 4MAT and the four quadrants, they realized that all the steps in their process fell into Quadrants Two and Three. I asked them what they had learned that would enable them to design a more effective plan if they were to try again. The following wheel is the result of their new thinking and planning:

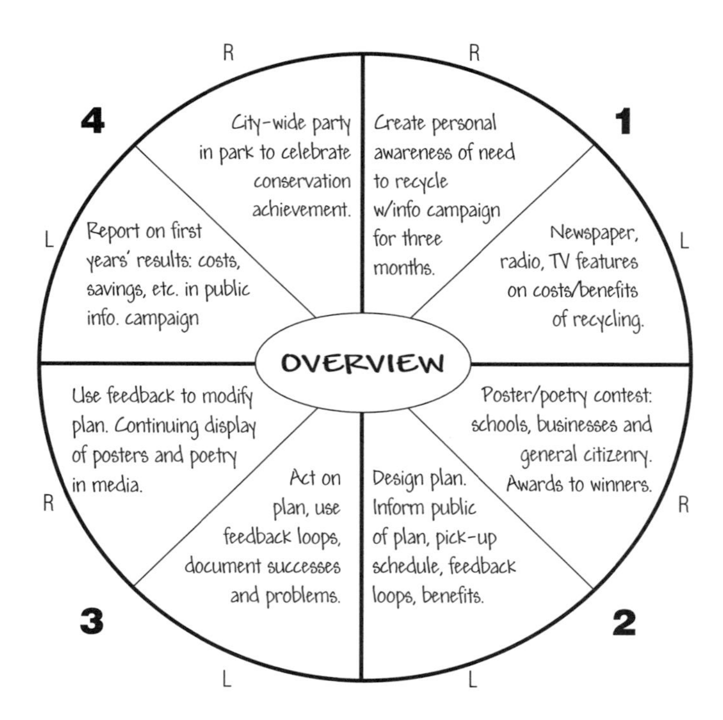

Quadrant One, R Mode

The city invests in a public education campaign to inform citizens about the why of recycling. This campaign includes TV and radio spots, newspaper features, and discussion at local citizen action meetings and in the City Council.

Quadrant One, L Mode

The city informs citizens of the costs and benefits of recycling, with adequate information about the types of materials that are to be recycled the first year of the program.

Quadrant Two, R Mode

The city sponsors a poster/poetry contest and invites school children, employees of area businesses, and the general citizenry to submit entries which tout the benefits of recycling with an emphasis on conservation. The city invites local businesses to provide awards for the winners and advertises the winners in the local media.

Quadrant Two, L Mode

The city creates the actual plan including types of materials to be recycled, by what businesses, at what cost, pick-up schedules, a letter explaining the pick-up system and carefully identifying what can and cannot be picked up. The city involves members of local citizen action committees in the choice of recycling containers which the city then purchases and delivers to the citizens. A feedback plan is created and put in place with appropriate staff.

Quadrant Three, L Mode

The plan is implemented and the feedback loops are used. Successes and problems are documented for immediate attention.

Quadrant Three, R Mode

Feedback is used to modify the plan as the implementation progresses. Local media continue to unveil poster and poetry entries to keep the recycling issue in the public eye.

Quadrant Four, L Mode

The city prepares a report at first year-end on the costs and benefits and lessons learned during the first year. The report is made public and summaries are carried by local media. The city is careful to note changes in the plan based on citizen feedback.

Quadrant Four, R Mode

The city sponsors a celebratory event, such as a parade or an award ceremony, to tout the achievements of the first year of the program. Communities and/or individuals who made contributions are featured. The city announces that some of the proceeds from the savings of the first year will be spent on tree planting and public seating for the city's parks.

An Accreditation Plan for Statewide Training Schools

When I was at a state Division of Youth Services, I was the overseer of five training schools for adjudicated juvenile delinquents. The Executive Management Team of which I was a member decided to apply to the American Correctional Association for accreditation of the five schools.

At that time, less than eight percent (8%) of the training schools in the country had applied for accreditation because the standards were considered difficult to attain. The process takes three years.

The process was put on a 4MAT wheel. It worked. All five schools received accreditation, none with a ranking of less than 96%.

Three-Year Accreditation Application to the American Correctional Association by a Statewide System of Training Schools for Adjudicated Juvenile Delinquents.

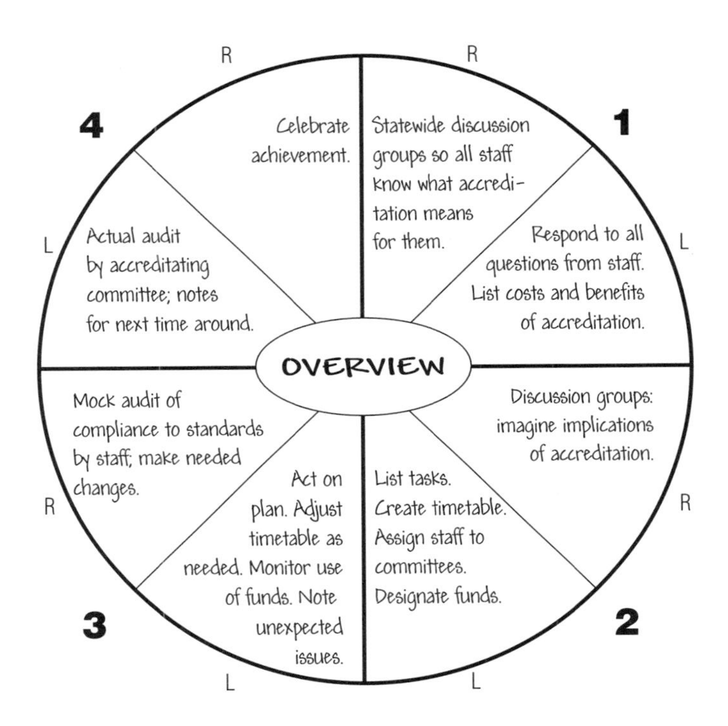

Quadrant One, Right and Left Modes and Quadrant Two, Right Mode take up the first year of the three-year process, testifying to the importance of beginning with the people needs. Management makes announcements, releases correspondence, and sponsors discussion groups so that every employee in every institution has a personal awareness of the meaning of the ACA accreditation. Questions from staff are noted and answered. Staff are taken through imaginary scenarios in which they can examine the value of accreditation to themselves, to the young people they supervise, and to their institution.

Quadrant Two, L Mode

The actual plan for complying with the 400-plus standards is written. Work is assigned to committees made up of specific staff. A timetable for compliance of each standard is determined. Necessary funds are designated.

Quadrant Three, L Mode

The plan is implemented. Unexpected issues and problems are noted and handled. Adjustments are made as necessary in work assignments, budget allocations, and timetables. Quadrant Two, Left Mode and Quadrant Three, Left Mode take one and one-half years.

Quadrant Three, R Mode

Local staff comprise mock audit teams and check their own institutions for compliance to standards. Needed changes are made.

Quadrant Four, L Mode

Actual audits are conducted by accreditation teams. Notes are made and filed for reference for future accreditation applications.

Quadrant Four, R Mode

There are celebrations held on each campus and in the central office of the accreditations. Local businesses contribute resources for a dinner for staff and students

Bibliography

Authors whose work strongly influenced this book

Anderson, Sherwood. *Winesburg, Ohio.* New York: Modern Library, 1919.

Bateson, Gregory. *Mind and Nature: A Necessary Unity.* New York: Bantam Books, 1979.

Belenky, Mary Field, Blythe McVicker Clinchy, Nancy Rule Goldberger and Jill Mattuck Tarule. *Women's Ways of Knowing: The Development of Self, Voice, and Mind.* New York: Basic Books, 1986.

Berlin, Isaiah. *The Hedgehog and the Fox.* Chicago: Ivan Dee, 1953.

Bruner, Jerome S., Rose R. Olver, Patricia M. Greenfield et al. *Studies in Cognitive Growth, A Collaboration at the Center for Cognitive Studies,* New York: John Wiley and Sons, Inc., 1966.

Dewey, John. *Art as Experience.* New York: G.P. Putnam, 1934.

Dewey, John. *Experience and Education.* Kappa Delta Pi, 1938.

Diamond, Marian Cleeves. *Enriching Heredity: The Impact of the Environment on the Anatomy of the Brain.* New York: The Free Press, l988.

Eisner, Elliot W. "The Role of Education in the Cultural and Artistic Development of the Individual." *Recent Papers,* Palo Alto: Stanford University, School of Education, 1992.

Gould, Stephen Jay. *The Mismeasure of Man.* New York: W.W. Norton, 1981.

Greene, Maxine. *Releasing the Imagination: Essays on Education, the Arts, and Social Change.* San Francisco: Jossey-Bass, 1995.

Howe, Harold II. *Thinking About Our Kids: An Agenda for American Education.* New York: The Free Press Inc., 1993.

Jones, Richard. *Fantasy and Feeling in Education.* New York: New York University Press, 1968.

Kegan, Robert. *In Over Our Heads: The Mental Demands of Modern Life.* Cambridge, MA: Harvard University Press, 1994.

Kegan, Robert. *The Evolving Self: Problem and Process in Human Development.* Cambridge, MA: Harvard University Press, 1982.

Kincheloe, Joe L. and Shirley R. Steinberg. "A Tentative Description of Post-formal Thinking: The Critical Confrontation with Cognitive Theory." Cambridge, MA; *Harvard Educational Review,* Vol 63, No. 3, Fall, 1993.

Kolb, David A. *Experiential Learning: Experience as the Source of Learning and Development.* Englewood Cliffs, NJ: Prentice-Hall, 1984.

Lewis, C. S. *God in the Dock: Essays on Theology and Ethics.* Walter Hooper, Ed. Grand Rapids, MI: William B. Erdmans Publishing, 1970.

Macmurray, John. *The Structure of Religious Experience.* New Haven, CT: Yale University Press, 1936, reprint, 1971.

Maslow, Abraham. *Toward a Psychology of Being.* 2nd Ed. New York: Van Nostrand Reinhold Company, 1964.

Moore, Thomas. *Thomas Moore on Creativity, Parts One and Two Audio Tapes.* Boulder, CO: Sounds True Recordings, 1993.

Moustakas, Clark. *Creativity and Conformity.* New York: D. Van Nostrand, 1967.

Nicoll, Maurice. *Psychological Commentaries on the Teaching of Gurdjieff and Ouspensky.* Boston: Random House, 1980.

Nietzsche, Friedrich. *The Will to Power.* Translation, W. Kaufmann and R.J. Hollingdale. Ed. W. Kaufmann. London: Weidenfeld and Nicolson, 1967.

Noddings, Nel. "A Morally Defensible Mission for Schools in the 21st Century," Bloomington, IL: *Phi Delta Kappan,* Vol. 76, No. 5, Jan. 1995.

Peat, F. David. *Synchronicity: The Bridge Between Matter and Mind.* New York: Bantam Books, 1987.

Polanyi, Michael. *The Tacit Dimension.* Gloucester, MA: Peter Smith, 1983.

Rorschach, H. *Psychodiagnostics.* 5th ed. Translated by P. Lemkau and B. Kronenberg. Berne, Switzerland: Verlag Han Huber, 1951.

Schopenhauer, Arthur. *The World as Will and Representation.* Translated by E. F. J. Payne, Vols. I and II. NY: Dover, 1966.

Shlain, Leonard. *Art and Physics: Parallel Visions in Space, Time and Light.* New York: Morrow, 1991.

Thelen, Herbert. *Education and the Human Quest.* NY: Harper, 1960.

West, Thomas G. *In The Mind's Eye: Visual Thinkers, Gifted People with Learning Difficulties, Computer Images, and the Ironies of Creativity.* Buffalo, New York: Prometheus Books, 1991.

Whyte, David. *The Heart Aroused: Poetry and the Preservation of the Soul in Corporate America.* NY: Currency, Doubleday, 1994.

Brain

Bruner, Jerome S. *On Knowing: Essays for the Left Hand.* Cambridge, MA: Harvard University Press, 1962.

Caine, Renata and Geoffrey Caine. *Teaching and the Human Brain.* Alexandria, VA: Association for Supervision and Curriculum Development, 1991.

Campbell, Jeremy. *The Improbable Machine.* New York: Simon and Schuster, 1989.

Cooper, L.A. and R.N. Shepherd. *Mental Images and Their Transformation.* Cambridge, MA: MIT Press, 1982.

Csikzentmilalyi, Mihaly. *Flow: The Psychology of Optimal Experience.* New York: Harper and Row, 1990.

Diekman, Arthur. "Biomodal Consciousness," *Archives of General Psychiatry,* 25, 1971.

Damasio, Antonio. *Descartes' Error: Emotion, Reason, and the Human Brain.* New York: G. P. Putnam, 1994.

Gardner, Howard. *Multiple Intelligences: The Theory in Practice.* New York: Basic Books, 1993.

Gardner, Howard. "Reflections on Multiple Intelligences: Myths and Messages." Bloomington, IL: *Phi Delta Kappan,* Vol 77, No. 3, Nov. 1995.

Healy, Jane M. *Endangered Minds: Why Children Don't Think and What We Can Do About It.* New York: Simon and Schuster, 1990.

Merleau-Ponty, Maurice. *Phenomenology of Perception,* translated from the French by Colin Smith. London: Routledge, 1989.

Springer, Sally and Georg Deutsch. *Right Brain, Left Brain.* San Francisco: W.H. Freeman, 1981.

Storr, Anthony. *Music and the Mind.* New York: The Free Press, MacMillan, 1992.

Strauch, Ralph. *The Reality Illusion: How You Make the World You Experience.* Barrytown, NY: Station Hill Press, 1983, 1989.

Learning Styles

Hunt, David. *Beginning With Ourselves: In Practice, Theory and Human Affairs.* Cambridge, MA: Brookline Books, 1987.

Jung, Carl. *Psychological Types.* Princeton, NJ: Princeton University Press, 1976, original, 1923.

McCarthy, Bernice. *The 4MAT System: Teaching to Learning Styles with Right/Left Mode Techniques.* Barrington, IL: Excel, Inc., 1981, 1987.

McCarthy, Bernice. *The Learning Type Measure.* Barrington, IL: Excel, Inc., 1993.

Wagner, Richard K. and Robert J. Sternberg. "Practical Intelligence in Real-World Pursuits: The Role of Tacit Knowledge." *Journal of Personality and Social Psychology.* Vol. 49, No. 2, 1985.

Wagner, Richard K. and Robert J. Sternberg, editors. *Practical Intelligence: Nature and Origins of Competence in the Everyday World.* New York: Cambridge University Press, 1986.

Worringer, Wilhelm. *Abstraction and Empathy.* Translation, M. Bullock. London: Routledge and Kegan Paul, 1963.

Pedagogy

Ashton, Patricia Teague, editor "Constructivist Approaches to Teacher Education," *Journal of Teacher Education* Vol. 43, No. 5, Nov-Dec, 1992.

Bruner, Jerome S. *The Process of Education.* Cambridge, MA: Harvard University Press, l960.

Bruner, Jerome S. *Toward a Theory of Instruction.* Cambridge, MA: Belknap Press of Harvard University, 1966.

Eisner, Elliot W. *The Enlightened Eye: Qualitative Inquiry and the Enhancement of Educational Practice.* New York: Macmillan, 1991.

Freire, Paulo. *Pedagogy of the Oppressed.* New York: The Continuum Publishing Corporation, 1987. Originally published in 1970.

Furth, Hans G. *Piaget for Teachers.* Englewood Cliffs, NJ: Prentice-Hall, 1970.

McCarthy, Bernice and Susan Morris. *4MAT in Action, Sample Units for Grades K-6.* Barrington, IL: Excel, Inc., 1995.

McCarthy, Bernice and Susan Morris. *4MAT in Action, Sample Units for Grades 7-12.* Barrington, IL: Excel, Inc., 1995.

Piaget, Jean and B. Inhelder. *The Psychology of the Child.* New York: Basic Books, 1969.

Sizer, Ted. "What's Wrong with Standardized Tests?" New York: *The New York Times,* Jan. 8, 1995.

Sizer, Ted. *Horace's Compromise: The Dilemma of the American School.* Boston: Houghton Mifflin, 1984.

Sizer, Ted. *Horace's School: Redesigning the American High School.* Boston: Houghton Mifflin, 1992.

Vygotsky, L. S. *Mind in Society.* M. V. Cole, J. Steiner, S. Scribner, E. Souberman, Editors. Cambridge, MA: Harvard University Press, 1978.

Whitehead, Alfred North. *Aims of Education and Other Essays.* New York: Macmillan, 1929.

Wiggins, Grant P. *Assessing Student Performance: Exploring the Purpose and Limits of Testing.* San Francisco: Jossey-Bass, 1993.

Management

Deal, E. Terrence and Lee G. Bolman. *Reframing Organizations: Artistry, Choice, and Leadership.* San Francisco: Jossey-Bass, 1991.

Deal, Terrence E. and Kent D. Peterson. *The Leadership Paradox: Balancing Logic and Artistry in Schools.* San Francisco: Jossey-Bass, 1994.

Drucker, Peter. *The Effective Executive.* NY: Harper and Row, 1966.

Greenleaf, Robert K. *Servant Leadership: A Journey into the Nature of Legitimate Power and Greatness.* New York: Paulist Press, 1977.

Lewin, Kurt. *Field Theory in Social Sciences.* New York: Harper and Row, 1951.

McCarthy, Bernice and Suzanne Sanders. *The Leadership Behavior Indicator.* Barrington, Il: Excel, Inc., 1989.

Norman, Donald A. *The Design of Everyday Things.* New York: Doubleday, 1988.

Peters, Thomas J. and Robert H. Waterman, Jr. *In Search of Excellence.* New York: Harper and Row, 1982.

Peters, Thomas. *Thriving on Chaos: Handbook for a Management Revolution.* New York: Alfred A. Knopf, 1988.

Sculley, John. *Odyssey: Pepsi to Apple, A Journey of Adventures, Ideas and the Future.* New York: Harper and Row, 1987.

Senge, Peter M. *The Fifth Discipline.* New York: Doubleday, 1990.

Index to Authors